101 No Cost (And Low Cost) Techniques Turbo Charge Your Freelance Income

Beth Ann Erickson

101 No Cost (And Low Cost) Techniques To Turbo Charge Your Freelance Income

Beth Ann Erickson

101 Low Cost/No Cost...

Beth Ann Erickson

101 No Cost (And Low Cost) Techniques Turbo Charge Your Freelance Income

101 Low Cost/No Cost...

A Note From Beth:

Hi. I'm Beth Ann Erickson, an actual working writer. I write copy for businesses, corporations and nonprofit organizations. I've written hundreds of articles for newspapers, newsletters, and nationally distributed magazines. I'm polishing my sixth book as I write this.

I hold a bachelors degree in Communications and Sociology. I even attended Sorbonne University in Paris one summer. (Boy, that was an experience of a lifetime!)

This past year, my latest "business partner" died. She was my "Lucy the Rat Terrier Wonder Dog." Today I write with Cutie Rudie the Doxie Cross and Jake, the Min-Pin. They're living up to their job titles as "Official Filbert Publishing Muses." I've come to love both of them....

So here's my point. If I can live in the middle of nowhere and make a GREAT living writing, there's no reason why you can't. All it takes is a little know-how and practice. And that's exactly what you'll get with "101."

So roll up your sleeves. Get ready to write. Get ready to have fun.

And if you like "101," be sure to subscribe to my free e-mag. Each week, you'll receive tips, techniques, and inspiration to keep your keyboard humming. Check it out at http://filbertpublishing.com/.

Beth's books include:

Jumpstart Your Writing Career – and Snag Paying Assignments
The Almach – A Novel
HeartSongs – A Novel
How to Get Happily Published Without Falling For Scams, Hooks, Lines, and Sinkers.

Upcoming Titles

The Honest Businessperson's Guide to Writing Awesome Advertising
TGV – A Novel
Murder on Third – A Novel

Make your writing sparkle. Write killer queries. Get published. Subscribe to Writing Etc. the free e-mag for writers. Receive the free e-booklet "Power Queries" by subscribing today. http://filbertpublishing.com/

Beth Ann Erickson

101 No Cost (And Low Cost) Techniques To Turbo Charge Your Freelance Income

Filbert Publishing

Table of Contents

Introduction

Whenever I ask a writer, "What was the one aspect of running your business that surprised you the most," the answer is nearly universal.

"I never expected to have to promote so much."

Depending how you look at it, fortunately or unfortunately... if you're going to be a successful writer, you're going to HAVE to promote yourself.

Books won't move off your storage shelves without a half-decent marketing plan. Potential clients will not know you exist without some savvy marketing on your part.

In fact, it may sound downright brazen, but without solid marketing skills on your part, you simply will not make a living as a writer. The more developed your marketing skills, the more you'll sell. Period.

After all, consider this:

Last weekend I worked on this quarter's royalty statements for our authors.

Now, I rarely pull back the curtain and write about something as intimate as our author's earning. However, rest assured, I won't reveal any specifics. Nor will I name names.

But the information I unearthed while cutting those checks just may transform your writing career.

Here's what I observed:

Calculating royalties is always interesting. Whenever we receive payment for a book, we instantly record the author's royalty on a grid. As the quarter progresses, the numbers mount. Finally a few days before the end of a quarter, our computer tallies the totals, we print statements, then cut the checks.

Pretty easy system.

What's interesting about this method is that we can actually track the effects of our author's marketing efforts.

For example, I was speaking with one of our authors and he/she mentioned that they'd purchased a particular book marketing program.

"Do you think it'll work?"

"Give it a try," I replied. "I'll e-mail if we see a spike in sales."

Within a week, both Baker and Taylor and Amazon contacted us requesting more copies of their book. Plus we'd received sales directly from our site.

Was the marketing program a success?

It's hard to say. I don't know what he/she paid for it. But I can say that their book sales spiked, then leveled off far higher, selling more books per month than before they purchased the program.

In that respect, the program paid off in spades. Plus this author's not only a great writer, they're now a far savvier marketer.

On the other hand, the authors who don't actively apply marketing skills to their writing career... well unfortunately they either received utterly puny checks or (horror or horrors) no check at all.

Nixie. Nada. Rien.

The chasm's huge. A fat, hearty check or zip.

Acquiring a large readership or allowing your work to languish in obscurity.

Allowing your thoughts free flight versus laboring their release and watching them fall flat.

And that, my friend, vividly illustrates every successful writer's secret weapon: Marketing savvy.

Think I'm wrong?

Ponder the top selling fiction today. Is the writing perfect? Fantastic, original plots?

Sometimes, perhaps. But on the whole, most top selling fiction is pure bologna.

But successful authors are effective marketers right down to the bone.

And that's when your job gets interesting.

You see, as you read this, you probably have at least as much talent as some of the most successful writers today. And if your checks aren't as healthy as you'd like them to be, what you probably lack is marketing expertise.

The actual act of writing is a learned skill. It's developed through study and taking time to voraciously read whatever it is you want to write.

For example, if you want to write novels, you must read novels. If your goal is to write direct mail, you've gotta read a ton of it. Love nonfiction? You guessed it, you've got to read nonfiction until it's oozing from your pores if you hope to become the best in your genre.

But if you desire to become the kind of writer who touches the heart of multitudes, you need to add a few marketing skills to your writing arsenal.

It's a sad truth that even the best writing won't get read without effective marketing backing it up.

While driving to St. Cloud last weekend in my son's new car, the radio blared a goldie oldie.

"Ugh," my son grunted, "Who's that awful singer. She's gonna pop my ear drums."

I chuckled at his comment and answered, "That's Madonna."

Now, please realize that this particular song certainly wasn't this artist's best work. It was kinda old… didn't translate well into this particular 17 year old's mind. But seriously, this song was mucho nasal.

"No way," Peder (my dear son) gushed. "Madonna? You've gotta be kidding. I've never heard her sing before, but boy does she suck. I can't believe people listen to her music."

"Yeah, she's still popular," I replied. "Marketing's a big reason for her success."

Peder rolled his eyes, "Well she didn't make it on singing talent alone…."

Now, you may or may not agree with Peder's assessment of Madonna's vocal talents. But I think we can all agree that the woman's one of the most skilled marketers today.

Which leads me to my next point.

Now's a perfect time to harness this incredible force yourself and really launch your writing career.

After all, promotion's not that bad – at least not after you understand how it works. There are countless techniques you can use and the list I provide in this book is hardly exhaustive.

Simply stated, the more creative you get in self-promotion, the more business you'll generate and the more success you'll experience. It's as simple as that.

So use this book as a jumping-off point. Use the ideas that work for you. Chuck the ones that suck. Then expand on every idea that rings true for you. But most of all… have fun.

And keep me posted on how it's going! You can always find me at http://filbertpublishing.com or shoot an e-mail to mailto:filbertpublishing@filbertpublishing.com

Let's get started, after all, this is your career we're talking about. So here they are… 101 Low and No Cost Techniques to Supercharge Your Writing Income:

Getting Started….

If you're a newbie writer, I'm starting with the ideas, tips, and what-have-yous, that will lay the foundation for your success. And if you're already an established writer, taking a moment to review this section just may reignite some of the passion you had when your career was in its infancy.

I'll begin this section with a few assumptions. First, I'm assuming you're a competent writer. I'm also assuming that because you want to earn a living wage, you're willing to learn some of the secrets of writing ad copy, otherwise known as copywriting.

Becoming a competent… or perhaps even a skilled… copywriter will be the one of the most lucrative skills you'll develop as a writer, bar none.

Mastering the elements of persuasion will not only help you sell your novel, article, or poem, using those same skills to help business sell their products or services will jumpstart your income to (sometimes) unbelievable levels.

It's common for me to be able to charge a few hundred dollars per hour on a copywriting assignment that the client is more than happy to pay. After all, when my writing can pull in thousands of dollars, why wouldn't my clients pay top dollar for ads that pull like mad.

So… newbies, read this section carefully to prepare for success.

Veterans… scan this section and see if you can glean something that will make your business more efficient and profitable.

1. Prepare yourself for success.

Here's where you can *really* get the edge in your freelance writing career.

Take a look at any profession. Teachers must continue to earn Continuing Education Units to keep their license current. Sheet Metal Workers take classes on a regular basis to keep up to date with new government guidelines. (I know this because my husband is a sheet metal worker. ☺) Electricians must continually take classes to renew their licenses.

Freelancers who don't continue their education will become shallow, ineffective, and very poor writers.

We need to be curious. We need a zest for life. We need to wonder *why* something is the way it is.

If you're going to be a life-long freelancer, you must become a life-long learner.

Take classes. Not just writing classes… take FUN classes. I once took an Abnormal Psych class because it sounded interesting. I used the knowledge from that class when I wrote Heart Songs, my second novel.

Purchase and read books. I'm a reference book junkie. I haunt flea markets, book stores, and thrift joints…and never walk out empty handed. Read everything and anything. You never know when an awesome idea will flit on your shoulder. Fiction, nonfiction, how-to… doesn't matter. Read. A lot.

Subscribe to magazines. Writer's Digest. Home and Garden. Maximum PC. The National Enquirer. Mad. Vegetarian Times. Doesn't matter. Whatever remotely interests you… read about it.

Subscribe to e-magazines. Many are free.

E-mags will keep your finger on the pulse of what's new and hot. Paper mags often have a long waiting period between when they accept an article and when it finally runs. E-mags tend to be cutting edge with the newest information possible. Read quality e-mags to get a sense of what the paper mags will be running in a few months.

Now, I know you're a writer. So, why do I suggest that you read so much?

Simple. Stephen King in his book, *On Writing* explains it best: If you don't have time to read, you don't have the time or the tools to write.

The best writers are voracious readers. If you want to be the best, read.

2. Write a business plan.

I admit it. I hate planning. Give me a written plan outlining my day and I'll actually go to great lengths to make sure I avoid each and every item on the list.

It's just my personality.

That's why I needed, and still use, a loose, flexible business plan that gives me a sense of how I want my writing biz to grow while giving me the freedom I demand from this business.

As for your plan? Make it as detailed or flexible as you desire remembering to give yourself specific goals to shoot for.

Here are a few things you should include:

What will you call your writing business?

Many freelancers just call themselves something like, "Beth Ann Erickson… Freelance Writer."

Some get more specific. "Beth Ann Erickson, Marketing Expert and Freelance Advertising Copywriter"

Or, how 'bout this? "Beth Ann Erickson, Freelance Advertising Copywriter and Consultant"

Some people (like me) use a business name. I'm known as "Filbert Publishing and Marketing."

The name you choose is totally up to you. Using your own name is an easy option because when you choose a business name, you'll have to fill out a number of legal forms explaining that you're "doing business as" another name.

When I began Filbert Publishing, I had a quick chat with my accountant to find out what I needed to do to make myself legal. I'd suggest you do the same thing.

Next, you'll need to decide what you'll write.

Do you want to specialize in article writing? Copywriting? Fiction? Nonfiction? Perhaps you're an aspiring poet.

I'd suggest that you diversify to keep as many income streams as possible flowing into the business. That way when you tire of one project, another fresh one is always waiting in the wings. Also, it grants a sense of security knowing that if you receive a number of rejection letters, you have other hot projects bubbling.

Some writers dabble in mail order by creating products and sending full fledged direct mail packages to thousands of potential customers. Others sell products over the Internet.

The sky's the limit.

That's why it's a good idea to take a moment to decide what you LIKE to write, what kind of writing can create the income you desire, and then decide what the majority of your time will be spent on.

Now that you know what you enjoy writing, decide who your customers will be. Make a list. Crack open the Yellow Pages… get your hands on a current *Writer's Market*… and get to work.

Next, you need to research fees. Beginning copywriters easily earn around $50 per hour in central Minnesota. The rates are probably different where you live… probably higher. Also, you can read the *Writer's Market* and find out what publications are paying for articles. Target the higher paying markets but realize you'll probably have to sell a few articles for less money so you can build your clip file or portfolio.

You can also contact local publications to find out what they pay their freelancers. If you get hooked up with a regular freelancing gig with a local newspaper you'll eventually get more clips than you'll know what to do with plus receive invaluable experience in the world of freelancing.

Decide where you'll set up your office. If you can't find a dedicated work space at home, perhaps you'll need to rent a small office. Also realize you'll incur more expenses if you move away from home. I've freelanced over ten years out of my home and wouldn't want it any other way… but some people do. So decide where you want to spend your writing time.

Decide whether you'll keep regular office hours. Will you accept business calls at 9:00 pm? Will you work weekends? What if you get a writing assignment with a tight deadline at 4:59 Friday? Perhaps you'll work with a flexible schedule… or maybe you want to work 9 to 5.

Choice is yours.

You also have to decide where the money will come from to finance this new business. Although freelance writing is a fairly low-expense business, you'll discover that it does require cash flow.

You'll need to purchase a computer, internet access, paper, toner/ink, pens, pencils, three-hole punch, stapler, paper for brochures, reference materials, books, magazines, file cabinets, insurance... just to mention a few expenses.

Before you begin writing for clients, make a complete list of everything you can possibly need to begin your business. Separate that list into sections labeled, "Supplies I need ASAP," "Supplies I need later," "My wish list."

Let this list "rest" a while, add to it, subtract from it, and reorganize it, then go back to it one last time before you head for the office supply store.

3. Set up your work space.

First and foremost, your writing area should be comfortable. Whether you work in an office or carve out a writing niche in your bedroom, make sure it's a place where you want to spend a lot of time.

When I first started freelancing I worked out of a room in my basement. I thought I'd go crazy. The tiny window barely let in any light. On nice days, I felt like I was missing out on knowing what was going on outside. On rainy days I felt like I was missing all the excitement of a great storm outside. Every now and then I'd watch a pair of legs walk by... that's how I knew someone was coming to visit.

Drove me nuts.

It didn't take me long to take over the entire front room of our rambler-type house. Today I have a large window in front of my desk. The huge picture window is directly to my right. Lucy (my Rat Terrier Wonder Dog and writing companion) lays on her table in front of the window.

Best of all, I don't feel like I'm missing out on anything. If Lucy goes ballistic, I just turn in my chair to see what she's barking at. I watch kids come home from school. The seasons change before my eyes. Best of all… I get to watch those wild summer thunderstorms form, rage, and dissipate… all from the comfort of my office.

Secondly, be sure you carve out enough space for your office.

Writing on your kitchen table is OK, but be aware that you'll need more room than you think. Submitting a writing assignment with tomato soup splotches on it simply isn't professional, it's downright unacceptable. Avoid this problem by keeping your work separate from your family life.

In fact, a dedicated work space is ideal.

As you grow your freelance business, you'll need plenty of room for reference books, reading materials, and magazines. You'll also want to invest in a computer and high quality printer. You'll also want access to the Internet (if you don't already have this).

The 'net is a gold mine of freelance opportunities. It's also a great place to find reference materials for your articles. Beware, though… make sure your reference site is reputable or you may be using faulty information in your articles. As a freelancer, it's imperative that you always protect your reputation by using the best resource materials possible.

But I digress… let's get back to your work environment.

Third, you'll need a couple of file cabinets. One will organize your article research. Once you research an article, keep your materials and recycle as much as possible. For example, if you write an article for Dog Fancy called, "How to Train Rat Terriers," you can use the same sources and write a new article for Family Circle called, "How I got my Rat Terrier to Behave."

This file will also hold all the correspondence you'll accumulate as you make your way through your freelance profession. Keep copies of your queries here. Keep your rejection letters and acceptance ones as well. Poke copies of magazines you plan on contacting in here along with any other miscellaneous communications that you'll undoubtedly receive.

The other file cabinet will be your "swipe file." This cabinet will house junk mail.

Junk mail!?

Yup. You read correctly.

If you want to make a good living as a freelancer, you'll need to learn to write for businesses. Start locally by keeping every piece of advertising you receive from local businesses. Study it. Figure out ways to make it better. Then contact that company and offer to write their next mailing.

Beginning copywriters (writers who write for businesses) don't have any trouble earning at least $50 per hour. It's a great addition to your freelance income and a wonderful way to finance other writing projects.

Finally... when you're deciding where to house your office, keep in mind you may want to have a place where you can "spread out." For example, when I'm in the middle of an assignment, I often have papers spread across the floor behind me... often five to eight feet worth. Whenever I need to check out a reference, I spin in my chair, grab the right sheet, and get right back to work.

I need a lot of space. Maybe you're the same as me... maybe your not. But think about this before you choose where you'll write.

Also, I like loud music playing when I write. I have a friend who demands perfect silence. I like having Lucy near by. My friend goes crazy if anybody's in the room with her.

Think about all these factors when you're deciding on where you'll place your work area.…

4. Do you want a logo?

When I first started writing I would have told you to forget the logo. It's an extravagance. It doesn't mean much.

That was before I got the Filbert Publishing logo:

I've had more FUN with that little chuck of ink than I ever dreamed possible.

I stick it on my business cards. It's on every book we publish. I house it on my letter head.

Check it out. Look at your book spine, or scroll to the first page of your e-book (depending on how you're reading this book).

And by golly… Filbert Publishing is gaining a bit of an image because of that logo. Customers instantly recognize us and have an already-formed image of who and what we are.

This logo is a small step towards establishing a "brand" for ourselves.

Now a quick note is appropriate: don't waste your time trying to establish a "brand" of some sort. In the writing biz, "branding" is a natural evolution as a result of smart marketing. Pouring money into establishing a "brand" is a total waste. However, becoming a recognized authority in your field is a very economical way of establishing your own personal "brand" without pouring money into ineffective advertising.

Simply be the best at what you do and you'll eventually create your very own "brand" name. Attach a little logo to that "brand" and you'll become a bit more recognized.

Now... back on track.

Although I doubt our "brand" will ever be as strong as a multi-national conglomerate, our little foray into creating a brand is certainly paying off in spades.

Consider a logo. Dig through your clip art to see if you can find an appropriate image. Make sure it's royalty-free and free for unlimited use. Always abide by any limitations outlined in the terms of service when you purchased the clip art. Then create your logo and keep it alongside every one of your promotional efforts.

You'll be glad you did.

5. Decide on your promotional budget.

Regular promotion = Regular work.

Let me repeat that. Regular promotion = Regular work.

There's nothing worse than just coming off a deluge of writing assignments only to realize you have no pending projects.

No matter how busy you are, it's imperative that you stick to the promotional plan you've developed.

That includes your budget.

Decide how much money you want to spend on promotion.

Now, promotion doesn't have to be expensive. You can purchase small ads. You can sponsor an e-mag targeted to your audience. Create a direct mailing and send it to a targeted list.

You can write articles and request a fat byline. Craft a press release that'll land you in the local media. Sponsor a small event.

The options are limited only by your imagination. Once you decide on your budget, get creative and have fun.

6. Decide on your time budget.

The best promotion is often free, money-wise. However, your direct cost will often involve a fair chunk of time.

Decide how much time you'll devote each week to promoting your business. Whether it's an hour a day (or more), the time you spend promoting will often pay you back many times over.

You can write articles, work on a book, contact potential clients, write a direct mail campaign, draft a query or two... just to name a few.

If you spend time to properly know where your targeted market "hangs out" you can strategically place ads, participate in news groups, or even get paid to write an article that'll drive clients straight to your door.

Advertising that's targeted like a laser on your audience always out pulls shot-gun advertising that attempts to garner the attention of the masses. Always shoot for extremely targeted ads directed straight to your carefully-chosen audience.

Time spent researching your market and writing articles strictly targeted to their interests will pay off faster than you can imagine. There's nothing like a well placed blurb about your business to jumpstart sales.

7. Study your competition.

You need to know who your competition is and what they're up to. After you identify your competition, you need to study their style. Find out what they're doing right, and identify areas where you excel.

If you're writing ad copy, find out who they work for and why they were hired. Find out what their weaknesses are and fill that gap.

For example, if a local ad agency writes newspaper ads with fab graphics, but their copy is weak, offer to help them with that particular need.

If a magazine has great content but poor circulation, study their current marketing materials and offer to write their next subscription renewals/offer and boost their subscriber numbers.

When you know who your competition is and what they're doing, you can better create a plan of action that has a better than average chance of yielding amazing results.

You can easily study your competition by getting on their mailing (or e-mailing) list. Subscribe to their e-mag or magazine. Order one of their products. If they're a fellow writer, call and ask for a client list.

Surf to appropriate websites and dig deep. Find out what they're doing right and where their weaknesses are.

Studying your competition is one of the most revealing bits of marketing research you can do. You'll learn a lot about them… and yourself in the process.

8. Decide who you want to write for.

What interests you? What markets have a lot of money flowing through them?

If you can meld an interest of yours with a hot market, you'll have a nearly easy time generating a nice income.

List your interests, then find out who needs this type of writing. Now you need to dig through *Standard Rates and Data* (you can find this book at your local library) and find out the popularity of your prospective area of expertise. Ferret out what kinds of money people are throwing into this market. If you see a lot of money in your prospective subject area, you're likely in a good market. If the people you intend on enticing to hire you or buy your products are used to getting freebies, there's no point on courting them.

Next, you need to decide if you want to specialize in a narrow subject or whether you'd rather be known as a "generalist."

A "specialist", sometimes known as a niche writer is someone who becomes an expert in a narrow subject. Robert Bly is a copywriter who writes about writing advertising copy. He writes for a very narrow market. He's a renowned expert and makes a very good living.

A generalist is someone who writes on nearly any subject. Anything from dogs to sewing machines... weather to child rearing, it's all fair game. It's pretty tough to find an expert "generalist" because these people usually don't become a "guru" in any field. However, you can make a very nice living as a generalist.

When you know who you want to write for, you need to study the format, the preferences, the jargon, the style. Read all the publications in that field. Get on mailing lists. If you're a copywriter, pinpoint the weakness in their current promotional efforts. If you can strengthen that weakness, you're one step closer to landing the job.

When you're first starting out, write some articles on spec. Do the same thing with ads and other promo efforts. Mail them a specific person in that company and see if they're interested in using it.

Be careful about writing on spec. You don't want to make a practice of writing for free. Only in very special circumstances… a client you really, really, really want to work for, a market you just can't break into, a spectacular project you otherwise wouldn't get a shot at… should you consider writing on spec. It's a dangerous practice to write for free. Use the spec assignment route ONLY in the more dire of circumstances.

That being said, always send your correspondence to an actual person. For example, if you send your query to "Filbert Publishing," chances are the wrong person will open it. It'll get stuck in a box, sit there for a few days, and perhaps after a couple weeks, it'll wind up on another desk. The correct person may (or may not) eventually get it… but it'll take a while.

On the other hand, if you read the Filbert Publishing guidelines… and perhaps read a few past issues of Writing Etc., you'd know you need to send the query to Beth Ann Erickson. I'd receive it, open it, and give it my immediate attention.

Also, when I receive a query that starts with the words, "Dear Sir," I know they haven't done their research. I'll scan the query, but I admit I don't read it as carefully as one that says, "Dear Beth" at the top.

Study your market and send them appropriate material. Get your letter/query to the correct person. When you do this, you've already made your query better than most.

9. Sharpen your writing skills.

A writer who doesn't write on a regular basis isn't a writer.

Now, when I'm talking "writing" I'm not talking about online chatting. I'm not talking e-mail correspondence either.

These activities don't count as "writing."

I'm talking about real writing: articles, ad copy, nonfiction, fiction, etc.

The best way to sharpen your writing skills is to write. And keep writing.

The next best way to learn ultra-effective writing skills is to read. A lot.

Forget TV watching in the evening (unless you're an aspiring screen writer, then TV watching is research). Your time is best spent enjoying the genre you're working on at the moment.

If you want to write ad copy, spend your evening reading fantastic, ultra-effective ads and direct mail letters. If you're a fiction writer, read fiction. If you want to write nonfiction, read nonfiction.

You can also sharpen your writing skills by taking classes. University classes are wonderful, however beware of over-academicizing your writing style. There are some great home-study courses as well. Community Education classes often cover writing techniques as well.

Eavesdrop on conversations. Try to capture dialects in your writing. Master a verbal writing style and you'll snag more readers than you can count.

The average American reads about the seventh grade level. We're an auditory audience weaned on television and raised on radio.

It's a sad commentary that great literature simply doesn't reach the masses today. That's because the language doesn't speak to readers who are so accustomed to auditory communication.

The good news for you is that when you train yourself to write in a conversational style, you increase your chances of creating a rabid following because to become a successful writer in this day and age you MUST connect with your reader.

And the only way to truly connect with your reader is to write using their words, their slang, their point of view. More on this in a bit.

This means you can toss out much of what you learned in high school English class. This also means you must become intimately involved with your target audience and know them up, down, back, forth, right, left.

The more time you spend sharpening your writing skills to match your reader's vocal style, the better and more effective writer you'll become. And the better writer has a greater chance of landing the assignment. Guaranteed.

10. Study how your potential customers speak.

You need to speak directly to your reader. If you don't do this, you'll lose them.

So, here's what you need to do:

First, understand that the average American reads at around the seventh grade level. This means you should forget using "million dollar" words. Understand that you certainly do not need to dumb-down your message, just use terms that are readily understandable.

The general rule is this: write like you speak.

Don't try to write in any kind of "literary style." Just communicate in the same way you would if you were sitting at a table across from your reader and speaking to them.

This means you'll probably break more than a few grammar rules. This means you'll probably start more than one sentence with the word "and." This means you'll probably be accused of being a bad writer by your high school English teacher.

Read everything you write aloud. If you need to breathe in between a sentence, shorten it. If you stumble, revise. If your mind wanders while your reading, pull the excitement level up a notch.

But you must do more... you must also become an effective communicator.

You need to study how your potential reader speaks, and write using their style.

This means you get to become a chameleon, assuming the persona of your reader.

For example, if you're writing a piece for an upscale magazine targeting professional businesswomen, you'll use a different "voice" (using different terminology and jargon) than you would if you were writing a piece for the National Enquirer.

If you're trying to sell fishing lures to avid sportsmen, you'd probably use a different voice than you would if you were writing a piece for PC magazine.

You're a wise writer when you research your market thoroughly before submitting a piece to a publication. Read their back issues. Study their direct mail campaigns. Chances are, they've perfected the voice they use and you can jump ahead of a ton of wanna-be writers when you study their materials.

Ah... writing isn't for the faint of heart, is it? It's a lot of hard (but fun) work. And the writers who recognize this increase their chances for success.

11. Accept that you'll have to ALWAYS promote.

Your freelance business is just that: a business.

You may be chagrined to find out that just because you're a fabulous writer, agents, marketing managers, and editors won't beat a path to your door. You need to make all these people aware of the fact that you have something valuable to offer them.

As a copywriter, you can do this by drafting a stellar sales letter promoting your services to local businesses. Get a mailing list from your Chamber of Commerce and start writing, revising, refining, folding, and licking envelopes.

You can also write an effective brochure to send to prospective clients.

Postcards mailed on a regular basis are a great way to keep in touch with clients as well.

Scour your local paper and find businesses that have an ad budget. If they advertise regularly, chances are they have a budget. See if you can get a little piece of it by writing effective copy for those ads.

Books like *Jumpstart Your Writing Career and Snag Paying Assignments* (http://FilbertPublishing.com) have a ton of ideas on how to promote your business.

You need to do the same thing when you're contacting agents, editors, and publishers. Contact them with a well-crafted query whenever you have a new project to present to them. Your *Writer's Market* should be tatters by the time the new update is released.

If you don't have a regular promotion plan, you won't have regular work.

Let me repeat that: If you don't have a regular promotion plan, you won't have regular work.

Decide how many queries you'll send out on a daily basis. Then do it.

Sending out one query per day is better than sending a batch and sitting back and waiting.

You get a rhythm in your career when you send out a set number daily. And never miss a day. Even when you have so much work that you can't see straight... send out your set number of queries.

Do the same thing for sales letters. If you want copywriting assignments, you need to send out those sales letters.

I send out a set number of queries and sales letters daily. Because copywriting pays better than articles, I usually send out more sales letters than I do queries. But I keep that number constant.

Oh... and always tweak your queries and sales letters. As your writing skills grow, so will your promo skills.

Don't expect perfection on anything you write. My first promo letter (quite frankly) sucked. But it sucked less than my competitions. That's how I started.

Since then I've poured thousands and thousands of dollars getting my hands on the best materials that'll give me the edge when it comes to competing for writing projects. And every dollar I spend on honing my skills pays back in spades.

Keeping your promo plan regular will keep your stream of work regular.

One way to begin is by writing articles. Send them to targeted publications that cater to the audience you're hoping to attract.

So this is where we'll start zeroing in on some low-cost and no cost ways to promote your writing biz in earnest: Writing Articles:

12. Write articles for consumer magazines and ask for a fat byline.

Consumer magazines can be a tough nut to crack. Competition is fierce and (as always) some mags tend to enjoy raining assignments upon their favorite writers. But when you land an article in one of these major magazines, you'll probably receive a nice chunk of change along with the prestige of saying, "I just got published in..."

So, if getting published in major mags is difficult, how do you increase your odds of getting that juicy byline?

First, start smaller. Don't start by shooting for the huge magazines. Build a clip file by writing for local publications, then regional, then move on to the national mags after you've mastered the fine art of dealing with local and regional editors. The education you receive at the local/regional level is invaluable when it comes growing your writing career.

You'll learn the ins and outs of this crazy biz and will make important contacts you can use as you step up on each level of your career.

Never underestimate the power of smaller pubs. Use them as an important part of your writing career and as a step to larger markets.

How do you do this? Easy. Just purchase a local/regional magazine (or newspaper), look for a gap in their coverage, then contact the editor offering to fill that gap. Speak to them via the phone or face to face. Blatantly offer to fill that gap (always speaking more about them and their needs rather than you and your needs) and watch for their reaction. Chances are, if you play your cards right, you'll walk away with a writing assignment. If you don't, be persistent. Generally speaking, the publishing world is horribly understaffed and will almost always welcome a hard worker into their midst.

13. Write articles for web 'zines.

If you want an almost instant paycheck and nearly instant credibility, write an article for an e-zine in your field.

So... you're probably wondering... what's an e-zine?

Simple.

An e-zine (also known as an e-mag) is simply an "electronic magazine." These "electronic magazines" are usually affiliated with the publisher's website.

For example, our website, FilbertPublishing.com, publishes a twice monthly e-magazine called "Writing Etc." We e-mail it (via a list-hosting service) to writers worldwide who have subscribed and confirmed their desire to join our list.

We generally run around two articles per issue, four per month, not including any extra editions we send to subscribers.

When you consider the number of e-magazines circulating throughout the Internet on a daily basis, you'll come to realize that these little electronic wonders gobble up an incredible number of articles.

That's where you come in.

Submitting articles to e-zines is a quick and efficient road to publication. When a traditional magazine often takes months to get back to you on your query, e-zine owners tend to get back to their potential author much faster... often within a few days. Also the lead time for e-zines tends to be shorter as well, meaning you'll see your words in print faster.

Will you get rich writing for e-magazines?

Probably not. But you will gain credibility, you'll earn pocket cash, and if you're smart, you'll start your own e-zine, build your own house list, and eventually generate income by sending offers to your list that will help them make their lives easier, their careers run smoother, and offer them one-of-a kind deals not offered anywhere else.

But we'll talk about that later....

14. Write articles for trade magazines. Target industries that interest you and you just may land a new client in the process.

Trade magazines are the unsung hero of the freelance writing trade. Robert W. Bly goes so far as to call it a "hidden market" that few writers target, yet there is some serious money and definite credibility to built in these publications.

A trade magazine is a publication targeting a specific industry. With little broad-appeal, these little tomes often have fewer subscribers than mainstream consumer magazines, but their targeted readership is a godsend to any writer who is hoping to build credibility in a particular industry.

For example, if you're hoping to establish yourself as an expert copywriter, a feature article in *Target Market* or *DM News* will do wonders for your credibility factor.

Name the industry you want to target, whether it's the pets, paper, boats, farming, beauty salons, dentist... you name it... very likely you'll find a trade magazine geared specifically to that market.

You can find a huge listing of trade magazines in the current *Writer's Market* or you can get the latest guidelines at WritersMarketOnline.com.

15. Write articles for local publication and you just may land some local clients.

Never, ever overlook local writing opportunities!

Writing ads, brochures, articles, and mailings for local businesses can become a real boon to your pocketbook.

Local businesses need effective ad materials... especially if they're already paying for ineffective ads filled with ineffective, unpersuasive writing.

Your local newspaper is probably short-staffed and needs a reliable freelancer to cover events they'd otherwise not be able to cover.

Contact these local businesses and let them know you can write awesome ads. If you're unsure of your skills, read Bob Bly's *The Copywriter's Handbook* and/or subscribe to Writing Etc. (http://FilbertPublishing.com) to get your copywriting skills up to snuff.

Chances are, if you've got some strong writing skills, know a bit about the psychology of selling, and have done even a cursory study of the architecture of persuasion, you can start writing advertising materials right away.

However, always study books, take online courses, do everything you can to make your writing skills as sharp as possible. Just because you're writing good ads, imagine how much more you can make when you begin writing awesome ads.

Pick up a few books, start reading, master the principles of persuasion, then hang your shingle.

16. Barter ad space for articles.

If you're freelancing for a local (or regional) newspaper (or magazine) and find your wages aren't acceptable, ask if you can receive the remainder of your usual rate in free ads.

Most publications will jump at this offer because they'll keep a valued freelancer happy and they'll be able to use up some of their remnant space in the process.

I don't know if you've ever watched how a magazine (or newspaper) is constructed, but I liken it to a jig saw puzzle.

The designer must carefully lay out each page, each element, until all the space is filled. However often, they find themselves with a square that needs to be filled. Rather than put in a silly "famous quote" or ad for the publication itself, why not place your ad there?

But you won't get that space unless you ask for it.

17. Write a regular local column – then work to get it syndicated regionally... or nationally.

Writing a regular column that appears in a local, a regional, or even a national publication will build your credibility. Credibility as a writer will open more doors than you can possibly imagine.

With your name appearing in front of your target audience on a regular basis, you gradually become the expert that they'll call when they need something written for them.

Make sure you include a strong byline at the end of every column you write. Make sure that your reader clearly knows what you write, and that you're available to write on a freelance basis.

Submit your columns faithfully for a while, then start working to get them syndicated. Once your work is appearing in a number of publications, your column income will rise PLUS, you'll have more potential clients contacting you.

OK. So how do you get the ball rolling on syndication?

You can self-syndicate by pitching your column to individual publications. You can find appropriate publications by researching your library's copy of *Gale Directory of Publications*. If an editor accepts your pitch you simply submit your columns following their guidelines, bill the publication, and then collect your fees.

Not hard, really. But if you syndicate to a number of publications, you can fast find yourself in the middle of a bookkeeping nightmare.

Your other option is to pitch your column idea to a syndicate. King Features, News America, and Tribune Media Services will act as your broker, pitching your column to several newspapers at once. You can find more syndicates to pitch your idea to at WritersMarket.com and the *Annual Directory of Syndicated Services* in the July issue of *Editor and Publisher Magazine*.

A note on syndication: competition is utterly fierce. It's in your best interest to do whatever you can to build a readership, some notoriety, a large clip file, and a slew of upcoming columns before you approach a syndicate.

As with all areas of writing, it's wise to start small, then grow where you'd eventually like to be. That way you can work your way through the growing pains and enjoy your success.

18. Cross Promote your other products in your byline, at the end of each book and/or in your articles.

You need stellar marketing materials. Sales letters, queries, all of it has to be as strong as possible so you'll make sales on a regular basis.

However, by adding just a few sentences at the end of each book you write.., at the bottom of each article… at the end of CD inserts… is an easy and very passive way to attract new customers to your writing business.

You never know who'll read an article you've written. You generally don't know who has read your books. Many people at least peruse CD inserts.

But when you make it virtually effortless for your readers to find you by providing a website address or business phone number in your byline, you increase your chances of getting hired to write something for one of your many readers.

Never miss an opportunity to promote your writing business, no matter how small the opportunity seems at the time.

19. Write a sales letter promoting your business and send it out on a regular basis.

Ok. Suppose you're a competent writer. Perhaps a more than competent writer.

You've studied the craft and feel you're ready to start soliciting clients.

When you're just beginning your writing career, drafting a generic sales letter you can use to initiate contact with a prospective customer is a real timesaver.

You don't need to get too fancy with this. Forget creativity. All the client really wants to know is **how you can enhance their bottom line**.

Using the AIDA outline, you can easily come up with a strong letter. AIDA's an acronym for: Attention, Interest, Desire, Action.

Here's how it works:

Begin your letter by writing something to attract the readers *Attention*. Use an interesting story, a startling statistic, a bold statement; anything that'll speak directly to your reader, pull him into your letter, and persuade him that he needs to read the rest of your letter.

Next, you need pull you reader in by keeping his *Interest* level high. This is where you need to persuade your reader that he needs his marketing materials as strong as they can possibly be.

In the *Desire* section of your letter, you need to prove that *you're* the best person to write compelling marketing materials for him. Provide testimonials, clips, whatever you have on hand that you can use for this section.

The final section of your letter will include a call to *Action*. Tell your reader what you'd like him to do. Tell him to visit your website, call today, send in a card. You can even promise that you'll send him a helpful booklet if they reply.

Believe it or not, many writers forget to tell their readers what they want them to do. When you include a strong call to action, you'll increase your response by a lot.

20. Write a personal letter to companies you REALLY want to attract.

So, you're reading your latest trade magazine and stumble upon a company that REALLY catches your eye.

When you find a company like that, comb through your generic letter and personalize it for that company.

A personalized letter stands a better chance of getting read... something you definitely want to achieve when you're contacting a company on your "A+" list.

Some companies are what I call "Mailable, but not apt to hire me". These include smaller organizations that may not have much of an advertising budget. I send these companies my generic letter.

However, companies that have a definite ad budget, companies that use promotional materials like brochures, ads, articles, letters, etc. most certainly deserve a personalized letter.

I'll research them. I'll read articles about them. Then I weave my new-found knowledge into a personalized communication still following the principles of AIDA.

21. Send out a specified number of sales letters every day.

Instead of mailing a flood of letters to your prospective clients, saturating every business in my target market, I use what I call the "drip" approach to sending out my letters soliciting writing assignments.

I send between three to five letters per day. Queries, sales letters, e-mails… doesn't matter. I send out my three to five every single day.

Whether they're my generic or personalized letter, or a query to a magazine. Three to five letters per day. Period.

This generates a predictable work flow.

If you'll remember, earlier I mentioned that regular promotion = regular work.

So, when I'm not as busy I'll send out a few more. When I'm swamped, I'll still send out three to five letters.

Just like clockwork.

22. Create a great brochure advertising your services.

I've discovered that business owners are terrible mind readers.

For some reason, just my telling them I'm a "copywriter" doesn't make them automatically want to hire me.

Go figure.

However, when I tell them, "I've mastered secret techniques that top copywriters use to generate millions of dollars for their clients… and I can use these same techniques for your product", then I get a raised eyebrow and often hear, "Tell me more."

So, when you create a brochure outlining the types of marketing materials you tackle, keep your client in mind, always clearly stating what hiring you will do for their bottom line.

Forget saying things like, "I write great articles." Your client's "Aunt Rachael" can probably pen a decent article herself. But to get it published and sell the thing? Whole different story.

However, you can restate that… make it client oriented… by saying something like this: Articles are a fantastic way to introduce your company to prospective customers. However, finding a writer with the skills to write effectively to a large audience can be tricky. Yeah… you can hire a local reporter who has extensive reporting skills. However, reporting skills can fall short when you need a strong article using gentle touch of persuasion to convey a veiled call to action. This is where a freelance copywriter can give your article the punch it needs to get your phones ringing and orders flowing in."

See how the above paragraph is slanted towards the client and away from you?

As you create the brochure outlining the types of projects you'll accept, you need to always describe your projects through the eyes of your client, answering his question, "What's in it for me?"

23. Gather testimonials and use them in your marketing materials.

When you've been writing for a while, chances are you'll start receiving kudos.

Here's an example:

"Great job! Your direct mail package more than tripled our sales. D.C. Texas."

Whether you receive these accolades via e-mail, snail mail, or phone, always ask for permission to use them in your promo materials.

Here's what I do:

I receive a "kudo." I immediately write (or phone) back and ask permission to use their quote. If I get permission, I file it. If I don't get permission, I don't use the quote.

Testimonials are a powerful sales tool that you shouldn't be afraid to use. Just get permission first. Oh... and never, ever make up a testimonial. A fraudulent testimonial can get you in BIG TIME legal trouble.

24. Make a circular with a tear-off phone number... post it where potential clients will see it.

A resume writer I know generates a TON of work by creating a one-page flier containing a headline, four bullets, and a call to action.

At the bottom of this little poster, she printed her phone number multiple times vertically, then used a scissor to create a snip between each of them.

This little fringe of phone numbers made it almost effortless for new graduates to contact her when they needed their resume updated.

The fliers cost her around one hour worth of work, plus printing costs (a few cents a piece). Each client generated around $300 in income. Each flier provided at least 18 potential clients.

Not bad, eh?

After she spoke to me, I told her to add a little tag line just before the phone number... something like "For a kick-butt resume call XXX-XXXX." Of course, if your market is a little more sophisticated, you'll need to refine that tag line a bit. ☺

If this sales technique would work with an aspect of your writing business, definitely give it a whirl. Simply ask permission from the organization that owns the bulletin board, post your fliers and you've got a new income stream.

25. Develop an effective business card and give them out whenever anyone asks for your phone number.

I didn't do this for a long time... and I wish I had.

The minute you've decided on your business name, you need to purchase some professionally printed business cards.

Yeah, you can supposedly print these little babies using your computer, but please don't do this.

Plunk down some cash and purchase those nice, thick, non-perforated, raised ink marvels and write off the cost as a business expense.

Your business card conveys your image, and you want your image to be that of a professional person who demands professional wages.

When your business card looks awesome, ALWAYS give it away whenever someone asks for your phone number.

You're dropping your dog off at the veterinarian and they need your phone number? Give 'em your card.

Your child's at the doctor's office and he'll "call you in a day or so to give you the results of that strep test...." Hand over a card.

I've received more writing assignments from those danged cards than I can count.

Nobody will hire you if they don't know that you're available to write their promo materials. Sometimes a good looking card is all you need to land a $900 assignment.

This month... purchase some good looking cards. And keep sending out your newsletter and mailings.

26. Create, rent or borrow an appropriate mailing list and send a direct mailing.

Suppose you're an expert on all things related to the coffee-house industry.

Yeah. It's a narrow niche. But it could be profitable if you can attract enough clients.

If you don't have enough coffee-houses in your vicinity to create a great copywriting income, you can approach a list broker and order a list containing every coffee-house owner in the country who has recently ordered supplies for their business.

It's true. You can easily order lists containing pretty much any demographic you desire.

If you're targeting local companies, you can rent a wonderful list of all the prominent business leaders at the Chamber of Commerce.

Brokers like Edith Roman Associates and American List Council can set you up with any list you can imagine.

You can even rent e-mail lists. But be careful here. Never, ever, EVER spam anyone. If you rent an e-mail list, make quadruple-sure that it's a double-opt-in list. Also make sure you rent this list from a reputable company. NEVER purchase a list on a CDROM claiming to contain "1.4 million legit e-mail addresses!"

Bad news.

The US government, local authorities, and your current (and future) ISP will not smile upon your marketing endeavors if you inadvertently spam anyone.

This is why I advise marketers to piggyback their electronic ad with an existing list. Ask a reputable e-mail list owner if they'd be willing to run your ad in their zine. Perhaps they'd do a solo e-mailing for you. But always make sure the list is double-opt-in and that the recipients know the mailer well.

No amount of marketing is worth getting called a spammer.

But snail mail lists? No spam worries here. Have at 'em and get ready for an adventure.

Once you receive your list you can create a killer direct mail letter and wait for prospective clients to contact you... perhaps following up your mailing with a number of phone calls.

Don't forget your local media

27. Prepare yourself for television interviews.

As a writer you've got an interesting job.

Depending on your field of expertise, there are times when you'll be asked to attend a television event.

Whether you're being interviewed, are a guest on a talk show, part of a panel discussion, or are giving a sound bite for the local news, it's always to your benefit to prepare yourself in advance for these spontaneous events.

If you're (for example) invited to be a guest on a talk show, videotape yourself in a similar situation and analyze your performance. Videotape yourself more than once.

What you're wanting to do is observe and correct any odd gestures that you're not aware of.

For example, I had no idea I tend to bite my lower lip while listening to questions. One look at a practice video tape and that stupid habit was instantly broken.

Get an idea of the image you'd like to portray on the small screen, then practice until your actions reflect that image.

Another goal is to attract new customers. You can do this by mentioning your website in the context of your answer to various questions.

This is where an easy website name is beneficial. For example, I can slip FilbertPublishing.com into an answer whereas if my website name was member.FilbertPublishing.aol.com, it would be a lot harder for the audience to remember.

It's pretty flattering to be invited on a television show. However, if your appearance doesn't generate any sales because you portray a funky image or forgot to mention a way for the audience to find you, then your appearance is a hollow experience indeed.

28. Practice for radio interviews.

Radio interviews are much easier than television interviews.

Imagine sitting in a warm studio chatting with a radio host, all the while generating orders for your books.

This is an entirely possible scenario thanks to the magic of radio.

Again, practice before you enter the studio. Tape record yourself answering various questions. You'll discover that most interviewers ask the same (or similar) questions. If you can master a coherent, spontaneous sounding, answer, you can have a lot of fun.

Also, remember why you're on the air. Although it's flattering to think that you're invited because of your blazingly wonderful personality, you're actually there to generate orders or find clients.

Mention your website, without sounding like a commercial.

Thoroughly establish yourself as an expert by providing thoughtful answers to questions.

You're not a celebrity so forget about being coy or cute. If you don't have a fine-tuned sense of humor, forget the jokes and instead strive for clarity.

But most of all, have fun. And always promote. Subtly, though.

29. Get yourself ready for print interviews.

Print interviews are awesome. They're usually relaxed. You have time to backtrack if you feel your answer is inadequate. Sometimes you even get to review the article prior to publication.

However, you still should anticipate the questions you'll be asked and mentally prepare some answers in advance.

If your interview questions come in the form of an e-mail, simply answer the questions, add any extra comments that you'd like to add, proof it carefully, then send them back to the reporter.

If the interview is a face-to-face one, it doesn't hurt to know something about the newspaper that's profiling you.

Do your research. Read a few issues of the publication before the big event. Take note of their writing style and strive to match your interview with their style. For example, you may not want to use the colloquial language for an upscale magazine targeting business professionals. On the other hand, colloquial language is just fine for a magazine with a more relaxed tone... say one geared towards PC gamers.

Another example: Even the clothes you choose to wear on the big day (be prepared for the accompanying photographer who is bound to snap your picture) will be influenced by the style of the publication. You don't want to wear a Hawaiian shirt when the rest of the people in the publication are wearing Armani suits....

So, once you know what kind of publication your dealing with, you can practice the questions you figure you'll hear, and mentally prepare yourself for those questions you're not ready for.

When you're hit with one of those, just smile, take a deep breath, and answer with all honesty and integrity. Then hope for the best.

30. Have a nice cache of portfolio items available at all times (Sample product, press releases, sample interview, photo, articles, fact sheet, brochures, business card, FAQ, testimonials).

After all these media events, you'll more than likely receive requests for your "portfolio."

Since you're selling your writing services, keep a file cabinet stocked with samples of your writing.

Whenever a prospective client calls asking to see your portfolio, all you have to do is walk to your cabinet, grab the pertinent clips that match what he wants written, and pop it in the mail.

This cabinet can hold copies of articles, press releases, some sample interviews, fact sheets, brochures, an FAQ (Frequently Asked Questions), copies of your generic letter, a sheet full of testimonials, and any incentives you've offered that you can throw in the mix.

Whenever a client calls, ALWAYS acknowledge your conversation with a follow-up packet of information. Give your client a few days to review the information, then follow up with a phone call if they haven't contacted you yet.

Be sure to harness the power of the Internet when it comes to promoting your business.

31. Create a web site.

I received a very interesting e-mail the other day. It came from an extremely talented writer who wrote something that went like this:

"On the advice of a "career coach," effective immediately, I am closing my website. At this point in my writing career, it's money better spent elsewhere."

I was stunned. How can a legitimate "career coach" advocate closing a website – especially when a website is a powerful weapon in every writer's arsenal.

As I pondered what she'd written, I could think of ten reasons why EVERY writer needs a website. Here they are:

1. Your website builds credibility. Having a website presence places you as an expert in your field. A writer who takes the time to write and maintain a website is a writer who takes their career seriously. Not only that, having a web address on your business cards looks impressive....
2. Your website is a wonderful place to house your clips. Every query you send out can provide your URL along with links to your clips. Face it... a web site is like a billboard advertising your writing services. It's available 24 hours a day, seven days a week, plus it provides more information about you and your writing than any query could possibly hold.
3. Owning a website makes applying for online writing assignments a breeze. Keep an updated resume on your site. When you query

online publications, place the resume URL in your query. Also include your home page. Then your site will do most of the work for you.

4. Keeping a separate page on your web site for various resumes gives your assignment searches flexibility. Create one URL for your resume that focuses on your article writing abilities. Create another one for your fiction pursuits. Maybe you want one web page solely for your copywriting achievements. Each page can hold links for corresponding clips. Creating multiple resume pages focuses your querying efforts like a laser.

5. Owning a website is inexpensive. You can easily find a reliable hosting company for as little as six bucks a month. Plus, the cost of owning it gets lower when you consider that the cost is tax deductible (if you use it solely for business purposes).

6. You can sell writing projects on your web page. Once you have a nice flow of traffic visiting your site, you can diversify your income by writing booklets, articles, reports, books... and selling them. You can even sell e-books and forgo the effort of packaging items, or running to the post office.

7. Maintaining a website creates a hub where clients, other writers, and potential customers can congregate and "meet" you. When you have a website, I'm sure you'll create an e-mail link on every page so visitors can contact you. Answer every e-mail you receive. You'll make invaluable contacts, you'll network with other writers, but most of all... you'll make friends. Writing can be a lonely profession. But not so when you have your own "cheerleading section."

8. A website may make you newsworthy. And when your name is in front of your potential customers on a regular basis, you're more apt to obtain their writing assignments. What's newsworthy? The answer to that question is only limited by your imagination. Make your site the best source of information your clients need and you'll find yourself newsworthy.

9. If you want to write books, using your website to create a message board, "e-mail list" or e-mag may make finding a publisher easier. Showing a potential publisher that you've taken the time to create an

audience for your subject, showing them that you've got a few thousand potential readers waiting for your messages on a regular basis just may tip the scales in your favor when it comes to considering your proposal.

10. Owning a website and attracting traffic towards it is a big step in acquiring a readership. Fiction writers will find attracting a readership invaluable. Post chapter samples of your newest project online. Request feedback. REALLY get to know your audience. You'll be surprised how your perception of who will read your work differs from reality. When you know your audience, inside and out, you can tailor what you write to fit their needs. Then everyone's the winner. The reader receives something they need. You'll sell you're writing.

As you can see, these are some very compelling reasons to own a website. But if these haven't convinced you, here's five more bonus reasons why you should own a website.

1. You can anticipate the questions potential customers will ask and provide answers on a FAQ page. You'll save a ton of time if you don't have to repeat the answer to the same questions over and over.

2. You can stay in contact with your readers. Have an area where readers/clients/visitors can sign up for updates, news, etc. Then keep in touch with them.

3. You may acquire international clients. I live in Minnesota. I've written articles for people in Europe. Folks from Africa have purchased my books. I know I wouldn't have met these people without my web site.

4. You can convey the image you want to project on your web site. Want to look like a small company? Fine. Create a page that makes you look warm, cozy, and local. If you want to compete with the "big guys" make your page slick, professional, and concise. It's completely up to you.

5. Finally, your competition probably has a website and is already landing e-assignments. Know your competitors. Write better than they do. But most of all, squeeze everything you can out of every

dime you put into your promotion efforts. Creating and maintaining a web site is a wonderful way to reach as many potential clients for just a little investment of time and money. Your competition already knows this. You should too.

But most of all, creating relationships is the key to succeed as a writer in this millennium. A website enables you to create a very nice relationship with every one of your readers. Writing is a solitary profession. Interaction with people I've met through FilbertPublishing.com has become an unexpected delight as I make my way through this crazy profession.

32. Burn your website onto a mini CD and use it as a business card.

Ok. I'm wandering through Best Buy the other day, perusing all the new computer-related gizmos. And there, stacked next to the standard-sized CDROMs sat a little stack of tiny CDs that were exactly the size and general shape of a business card. They even came with plastic sleeves.

That got me to thinking... why not burn my website onto the CD? I could create a label that looked like a business card and include a mention that the recipient could pop the CD in his computer to see a full portfolio, FAQs, and group of articles he'd find helpful.

So, that's exactly what I did. I made a modified website and burned a bunch of my new "business cards". However, before I did that, I surfed the net to find a free html autoplay program that would automatically launch the site when the CD engaged.

With the CDs working properly, I proceeded to distribute them to prospective clients.

These little CDs are small, interactive, informative, and something of value that I doubt will get thrown out any time soon.

Give it a try.

33. No matter how busy you get, answer as many e-mails as you possibly can.

E-mails arc the bane of my existence.

Seriously.

They are the one constant in the freelancer's life that is both necessary and frustrating.

You'll receive assignments via e-mail. Reader questions will arrive in your in-box. You'll even receive an e-mail or two from someone who disagrees with something you've written. And then there's the never-ending flow of spam....

Whether you need to hire someone to help you with this continual onslaught or whether you answer them yourself always remember one thing: If someone has taken the time to send you an e-mail, it's always best to do you dead level best to answer it in a timely manner.

Easy to say, sometimes difficult to do.

Here's how I handle it:

Book orders and customer questions always get answered immediately. Potential customers inquiring about my copywriting services also receive an immediate answer.

Depending on the urgency, author requests (Filbert Publishing also publishes books) are usually answered in the order they come in, unless it's an urgent request.

Subscribers to Writing Etc. can expect to wait a bit for a reply to their e-mail unless it's urgent.

And chatty e-mails, without any questions or urgency wait their turn as well.

We delete all spam before it reaches the in-box.

I usually spend around one morning to one day a week just plowing through unanswered e-mails, however I'm on the verge of hiring someone to do this for me.

Believe me, as your freelance career grows, so will the e-mail flowing into your in-box. You'll have to decide at that time how you'll handle the constant influx.

34. Form an e-magazine and use it to promote your writing business.

One of the best bits of advice I received when I first started freelancing was to start an e-mag.

If you don't know what an e-mag is, here's a brief description: An e-magazine is similar in content to a magazine except it is only available in an electronic form. Our e-mag contains a couple articles, a short editorial, and some ads.

E-mags are released daily, weekly, bi-monthly, monthly... or any variation on those themes.

Some e-mags are free, some charge a subscription fee. Some are fancy and full of graphics, some are text based documents. Some are longer than long, some are less than one screen long.

As you can see, there's a great variation on this theme.

For a concrete example of what an e-mag looks like, you can surf to our website and subscribe to Writing Etc., our free e-mag for writers. If you're wanting to sharpen your writing skills and make a great living as a writer, you need to subscribe. Here's the URL: http://FilbertPublishing.com

So why would you want to create an e-mag?

Easy.

An e-mag will keep your name in front of any potential clients who subscribe. Whenever I work with a new client, I always ask if they'd like their name added to my e-mag list. If they'd like to be added, my name will appear in their in-box twice a month. It's rather difficult to forget who I am and what I do when they receive a twice-monthly reminder. Guess who they'll more than likely call when they need a writer for a project?

An e-mag is a great place to test new products that you're developing. Every new book I write is tested on my e-mag list before I plunk a load of cash into the project. If my target audience isn't interested in a particular project, why would I want to develop it further. On the other hand, if a new book receives a warm welcome from my test group, I'm almost certain it'll do well in the real world.

An e-mag is a money maker. You can sell products. You can sell ad space. You can join affiliate programs and sell other people's products for a cut of the retail price.

An e-mag keeps you in tune with your target audience. You'll find out what's hot, what's not, what works, and what bombs pretty quickly. Use this knowledge to make your and your client's ad efforts stronger.

To make sure your e-mail is successful in the long term always make sure that you use a double opt in system. This means that once someone subscribes, they need to respond to a computer-generated e-mail to officially get on the list. This one step will keep you off many spam filters.

Next, you need to keep your e-mag as short as possible. Send out a short message to subscribers telling them to click a link to get to the longer version of the e-mag on your website. Why do this? Again… spam filters. The shorter your message, the more filters you can avoid.

Lastly, invite reader involvement. Hold contests. Include immediately useful information. An active list creates avid readers. And as a writer, your goal is to cultivate a large readership.

An e-mag is interesting. It's not always fun… sometimes it's hard work. But it's always a new adventure. There's nothing like waiting to view the results from the latest mailing. It's very eye-opening.

35. Send out a "tip of the…."

If an e-mag sounds like too much work, send out a short "tip of the day" or "tip of the week".

Often only one (maybe two) screens long, these short gems aren't a lot of work and can pay off in spades by helping you establish credibility, attract clients, and sell some more of your products.

So… what kinds of products can you sell via these e-mails?

As a writer, you can sell your books, special reports, booklets, audio tapes, CDs, CDROMs… your product list is only limited by your imagination.

To sell your products effectively, all you need to do is fill them with indispensable information that your target audience needs.

It's that simple.

36. Host a survey.

Any time you can engage your audience in an activity, the readership of your e-mag will climb.

Find an interesting topic (or maybe controversial) in your field and solicit your reader's opinion on that subject.

Many e-mail list-hosting companies (like Yahoo and Topica) will allow your subscribers to vote on almost any subject imaginable. Request reader comments for even more participation then post/report your findings.

Another website specializing in surveys is SurveyMonkey.com.

The more interaction you can generate on your list, the more buzz you create. The more buzz you create, the faster your subscriber numbers will climb.

You can build a solid survey by surfing to other websites and noting how they construct their surveys.

Take part in a few.

Watch how the results are tallied and reported.

The best education comes from observing other writer's experiments, determining what's working and what isn't*, then adjust your plans accordingly.

*You can easily ascertain what is and isn't working simply by observing whether the author/website owner continues offering various types of surveys and by watching how many people participate in them. If a particular style of survey is repeated a lot, chances are, the website owner is having a fair amount of success with it.

37. Write articles... then GIVE them away.

Don't be afraid of giving information away.

I bet I've given out my first nonfiction title, *Jumpstart Your Writing Career* at least four times over in bits and pieces all over the Internet.

That little book also happens to be Filbert Publishing's fastest selling title.

Coincidence?

Nope.

Every time I dice out a chapter (or two) and offer it as a freebie article, it's invariably picked up by an e-zine and delivered to thousands of prospective book buyers.

Here's how it works:

I write the article/book chapter and post it on my website. I also submit the "freebie" article to any of a number of places where e-zine editors trawl for free articles. One such place is IdeaMarketers.com. You'll find a whole list of places to submit articles in Appendix A.

Be sure to include a nice bio with every article. Your bio should include a snippet of pertinent information about yourself (hook it with your article if at all possible) along with an effortless way for your reader to find you.

Here's my standard byline:

Beth Ann Erickson works as a freelance advertising copywriter. She's also the author of hundreds of articles, five full-length books, and is the "Queen Bee" of Filbert Publishing. Sign up for her free 'zine for writers where you'll learn to make your writing sparkle, help you write killer ads, and get published. You'll find all the details at FilbertPublishing.com.

Don't blatantly sell your books or writing services in your bio. Instead, push readers to subscribe to your zine. If you can get readers to sign up for your 'zine, you'll then be able to earn their trust and become the best source for whatever your subscribers are looking for.

Remember, your goal is to gain readers. Once you gain readers, you'll become a trusted source of information. Once you achieve this, you'll find it nearly effortless to sell your products or writing services.

Copywriting clients rarely contact me out of the blue. It's only after they've read one of my articles, surfed my website, and read a few issues of Writing Etc. that they pick up the phone and call.

Sometimes, once someone reads one of our freebie chapters, they'll surf directly to our site and purchase the whole book... but I find it far more beneficial for everyone when they sign up for the 'zine and we can establish a long-lasting relationship.

38. Create an online discussion group.

A big hurdle that many newbie writers face is that of credibility.

Sure, you can have your articles published. You can write books. But unfortunately, your potential audience/clients move quickly from one project to the next and will easily forget about how you can make their lives easier.

This is where an online discussion group can help.

An online discussion group consists of a group of individuals... your audience or potential clients... who gather together to discuss issues surrounding their industry/hobby/whatever.

A place like Yahoo.com often hosts these groups (for free) and will distribute these e-mail messages to everyone who has joined your list.

Here's how they work:

A member of the group reads something interesting pertaining to your subject matter. They shoot an e-mail to the group commenting on this article. Then other members pipe in and share their opinion.

And you, being the "owner" of the list will often offer your opinion as well... and will subtly establish yourself as an expert on this matter and will in turn, very quietly sell your services to your potential clients.

Sneaky, eh?

Yahoo takes care of all the logistics such as message distribution, dealing with bounced messages, subscribing, and unsubscribing, and all you do is help grow the list and keep an eye on the board to make sure everyone stays on topic.

If you want to attract clients, you need to target your audience, establish credibility, and then keep in touch with them on a regular basis.

A discussion group is an easy way to do this.

39. Hold contests in your e-mag (with your products/books/article booklets as a prize).

If you've been in business for any amount of time, in all likelihood, you've got a group of articles you've written, perhaps a booklet, maybe even a book you can use as a prize in your e-mag or discussion group.

I don't know of many people who don't love winning a contest, and as a writer, it's pretty easy to come up with a nice little prize when you have free information flowing from your fingertips on a regular basis.

All you have to do is decide what you'll give as a prize, then announce your contest in your zine.

Contests create buzz. Buzz will increase your subscriber numbers. Increased subscriber numbers will create increased sales.

It's that simple.

40. Create an e-mail chain letter.

This one can be tricky, although I have seen it work before.

Here's how an e-mail chain letter works.

Suppose you've got a great new freebie available on your website. You send an e-mail to your personal friends… perhaps a few zine owners… and ask them to pass on this valuable information to their friends and subscribers.

Then, in theory, they'll ask their friends to pass on this cool information. And before you know it, you've got a ton of people visiting your site and picking up your freebie. Oh, and did I mention they're also signing up for your zine as well?

Now, here's the down side. PLEASE READ THIS CAREFULLY. Never… I repeat NEVER try to sell an actual product using this method. If you do, you'll very likely be accused of spamming and will lose your ISP, your entire Internet business along with your reputation.

However, if you do have a great, valuable freebie such as a report, booklet, tip sheet, let your imagination run wild here, this method may work for you IF you only contact close friends of yours. A few zine owners may be inclined to give you some free press as well.

Used judicially, this method could bring some great clients your way.

41. Create a snappy e-mail signature.

Never send an e-mail message without including a short message advertising your business. You can easily set up your e-mail program to insert an e-mail signature at the end of every message you send. Just dig through the "help" section of your e-mail program and you'll very likely find step-by-step instructions to insert your benefit-oriented signature into every e-mail.

So… how do you go about writing a signature?

Here are a few basic rules to follow:

1. Generally speaking, keep it short. No more than seven lines is the industry standard. Make your signature longer, and you'll likely raise the ire of those e-mail recipients who are forced to slog through an over-long sales pitch.
2. Make your signature benefit oriented. Don't talk about yourself, write about what you can do for your reader.
3. Keep it simple. Don't try to advertise more than one item. I opt to promote my e-zine, Writing Etc. That way, if I gain a new subscriber, I can pitch our other products to them on a regular basis.

I once knew someone who considered themselves to be an effective marketer. They'd constructed a high-powered signature that hard sold everything from copywriting services to CDs to vitamins. Not surprisingly, that "power sig" didn't sell much of anything.

Don't make this mistake. Keep your signature simple. Ask for one and only one action on the part of your reader. If you have multiple books, send your prospective customer to your home page. Get 'em to sign up for a zine. But only ask ONE thing of your reader. Ask for more and they'll instantly ignore any direction from you.

That's basically it! Just for your reference, here's my standard e-mail signature that we've used for years:

```
Make Your Writing Sparkle.  Write Killer Queries.
Get  Published.  Subscribe  to  Writing  Etc.,  the
FREE  e-mag  for  writers.   Receive  the  e-booklet
"Power     Queries"     when     you     subscribe.
http://FilbertPublishing.com
```

Notice how the signature focuses on the reader, not on the zine. Also note the short sentences and the freebie thrown in for good measure. Also, see how it's easy to read, it's focused on one item, and best of all... it's short.

Now... this signature's been used for a long time. You may be wondering about ad fatigue.

Nope. After much testing, we haven't found a signature that beats this one yet.

Model your signature after this one and your sales will spike. Guaranteed.

42. Follow up with every e-mail prospect and ask if they'd like to be added to your e-mail list.

Whenever a potential client contacts me, I always invite them to subscribe to my zine.

There's nothing worse than losing contact with a client.

Because I'm a weenie who hates cold calling, I routinely use my 'zine to keep in touch with clients. I'm also not above contacting them via e-mail just prior to the release of the newest issue with something like this:

Hi Joe,

We're releasing Writing Etc. today around noon and I instantly thought of you. That's because I think the lead article will give you some great information that will help you as you prepare for the {fill in the blank} campaign that we talked about.

Just wanted to give you a heads up!

Enjoy your day,

Beth

```
Make Your Writing Sparkle.  Write Killer Queries.
Get  Published.  Subscribe  to  Writing  Etc.,  the
FREE e-mag  for  writers.  Receive  the  e-booklet
"Power  Queries"  when  you  subscribe.
http://FilbertPublishing.com
```

Note how this e-mail focuses on your client. Also note how the signature line fits in… the e-mail program inserted it automatically.

Keeping in touch with potential clients can be a breeze if you work smart.

43. Form alliances with other web site owners.

Writers tend to be surprisingly cooperative with one another.

I think it's because each project is so unique that although competition exists, it doesn't feel as cutthroat as some other industries.

When you set up a website, you'll be extremely surprised at how willing similar sites are to work with you.

FilbertPublishing.com works with multiple other sites. We swap ads and run them in our zines. We provide each other reviews for our products. We sell each other's products.

Working cooperatively is a win-win situation where your income has the definite potential to rise because of your exposure to potential new clients

Never be fearful of working with so-called "competing" websites. You'll quickly realize how networking can be a real boon for everyone involved.

44. Swap banners and links with other websites.

Every time a similar site to ours asks to swap banners and/or links, I'm exceedingly happy to do so.

Nearly every website has a page where they recommend other websites to their visitors. We used to call ours "Links that'll knock your socks off."

This page can be very valuable to you because every time you place a link on that page, you can request that the receiving page "link back" to you. If they do, you've got a potential new stream of new clients/customers.

A banner is simply a graphic that represents your site. We don't often use banners, but here's what ours looks like whenever someone requests it:

Make　FilbertPublishing.com
Your
Writing Etc.
Sparkle

We also submit our standard "blurb":

```
Make Your Writing Sparkle.  Write Killer Queries.
Get  Published.  Subscribe  to  Writing  Etc.,  the
FREE  e-mag  for  writers.  Receive  the  e-booklet
"Power     Queries"     when     you     subscribe.
http://FilbertPublishing.com
```

We also allow the website owner create their own description of our site. However everyone always includes your web URL so readers can click the link and land on your site.

Like I mentioned earlier, never fear cooperating with similar websites. I've never had a sour experience working and cooperating with fellow writers. I have a hunch your cohorts are the same.

45. Send "thank you" notes and article clips when appropriate.

Always acknowledge kindness.

I send thank-you cards all the time. I thank clients for their time after a meeting. I thank subscribers for their input. I thank our writers for trusting us with their books.

Taking the time to thank a client is not only good manners, it also sets you apart from your competition. Plus, if you take the time to occasionally send an article that you think your client will find interesting, guess who they'll think of when they need something written?

Hopefully you.

The name of the game is to keep your name in the forefront of your client's memory. You can do this by keeping in touch... hopefully on a regular basis.

Don't forget "real time" promotion.

Often your best customers, especially when you're first launching your writing business, are found right in your own backyard.

You'll undoubtedly find that competition is slight, if not nonexistent in your community. However you still have a few hurdles to leap over as you first begin.

Follow the following suggestions and you'll find that your promotional efforts will be far more effective....

46. Join civic groups.

OK. I know. These groups can be a real pain, especially for those of us who are hopelessly introverted.

However, if you're hoping to build a thriving writing business, you'd be savvy if you hung out where the movers and shakers of your community hang out.

This means you need to join your local civic group... or whatever they happen to call it in your community.

Here you'll meet civic minded individuals who are hoping to grow your community and probably own businesses themselves.

Once they get to know you and understand how you can help their business flourish, it won't be long before your telephone starts ringing with local business people asking you to write their promo materials.

47. Join your local Chamber of Commerce.

Here's where you'll meet the movers and shakers in your community.

From representatives from corporations in your area to local entrepreneurs and businesspeople, your local Chamber of Commerce is the meeting place for every one of these individuals.

Also, when you join your Chamber, you'll have access to the best mailing list of active businesses in your community. You may even reduce your mailing expense by piggybacking your mailing with a regular Chamber mailing.

Join your chamber today, get active, and find out how they can help you grow your business.

Which leads me to my next strategy...

48. Become an active member in your Chamber.

I'm sure you've heard this before and will probably hear this again: Your Chamber of Commerce can only help you build your business to the extent that you're willing to participate in their organization.

In other words, you must become an active member of your chamber if you hope to attract clients from their ranks.

Join committees. Offer to write for them. Network.

Promotion is an active and busy aspect of your business that you must take seriously.

That's because active, steady promotion = steady writing assignments.

49. Join your local arts registry/directory.

If your writing talents lean towards the more creative avenues, be sure to contact your local arts organization. Many of these maintain a directory where you can list your creative accomplishments along with your complete contact information.

Again, always remember when submitting your information to an organization like this, write it in a way so your bio will focus on you reader rather than yourself.

It's a sad fact that must be repeated... your reader doesn't care about you. They only care what you can do for them. Never forget this phenomenon.

50. Teach a university class. Teaching builds credibility.

It's easier than you think to apply for an "adjunct" position at your local university. Usually all you need is a bachelor's degree (and sometimes not even that) and a ton of experience in your field.

Pay isn't great, but the credibility you establish is worth more than gold.

Adjunct professors generally teach one class per term... often once per week during the evening hours.

The time commitment is fairly small and easily fits into most schedules.

Simply contact your local university or community college to see if they have the budget and interest in your field of expertise. Make sure you submit a proposed syllabus, lively proposal, complete portfolio, and updated resume. Also contact the university to check to see if they require any other documentation before you drop off the proposal package.

If you take care and submit a great package, chances are good you'll find yourself standing in front of a class and grading papers... and there's no bigger learning experience than teaching a class... as you're about to find out.

51. Teach an extension class.

An extension class is similar to a university class with the exception that you generally don't need a degree to teach it. If you're considered a solid professional in your field, you shouldn't have any trouble generating interest.

Contact your local university to find out what the requirements are for teaching these classes. Develop a great proposal and syllabus. Submit your materials and see what happens.

52. Teach a community education class.

This one's easy. Simply contact your Community Education department (this organization is usually housed within your local public school system) and pitch the class you're proposing.

Decide how many sessions you'll teach, create a brief syllabus, include any hand outs and wait to hear whether they'll include your class in their next session.

So... you're probably wondering what you'll teach.

Sky's the limit.

If you're a fiction writer, teach fiction writing techniques. You can also lead a fiction discussion group.

Nonfiction writer? How about teaching an article writing course. "How-to" classes are extremely popular.

If you're a copywriter, you can target your audience and teach a class on how to write effective ads/brochures/websites... see how busy you can become as a teacher?

I often teach a "How To Get Happily Published, Without Falling For Scams, Hooks, Lines, and Sinkers" class. I also teach a class for business owners called, "How To Spot An Ineffective Ad Campaign... And Turn It Into A Winner."

Choose your subject. Develop it. Then turn yourself into an expert by teaching a class.

53. Lecture to civic groups.

The name of the game here is to turn yourself into the local expert in your particular field. Once you're the established expert, work will flow towards you barely any effort on your part.

As I mentioned earlier, local civic groups are a great place to meet the movers and shakers in your community. When you give a short presentation to the local civic club, you have a chance to establish yourself as a knowledgeable and thoughtful professional to the very people who will someday hire you to write their brochures/ads/whatever.

Create a loose outline covering your main points. Whip together a few visual aids. Now practice your speech a few times.

Do NOT write your speech and read it to the group. Instead use little note cards to house your outline and step away from the podium.

If you're nervous, simply take a deep breath and remind yourself that you're presenting useful information that'll make your listener's life easier.

Then practice again.

Start by speaking to smaller groups and work your way to the larger ones as your confidence and skills grow.

54. Lecture to religious groups.

Business people come in all shapes, sizes, genders, and religions affiliations. Never hesitate to offer your speaking services to religious groups. If you can weave some of your own faith messages within your speech, that's fine… as long as they're complementary to the group you're speaking with.

If your faith isn't complementary to the group you're speaking with, simply omit your faith opinions from your speech and stick to your core message.

Don't try to convert anybody to your faith. Your goal is to simply provide fantastic business information to your listener and inspire them to take their business to the "next level".

And who can help them ratchet up their success? You, of course. By writing fantastic marketing materials, great public relations pieces, and helping them develop a positive public image.

55. Give presentations to students.

School funding is drying up. Teachers are desperate to find innovative ways to present information to this MTV generation that demands authenticity.

What could be more authentic than a weaver of words presenting a lively presentation to a Communications class?

Giving student presentations is one of my absolute joys.

Holding up direct mail letters and poking fun at some of the outrageous headlines (and explaining why they work... or don't work) makes for an incredible presentation that students talk about for a long time.

It's a win-win situation. The students get to peek into the writing life and find out why the skills they're currently learning in their classes are important.

You get a day out of the office where you'll build credibility, get an intimate view of an important and upcoming reading audience, you get a chance to polish your speaking skills, PLUS you'll have the time of your life. Guaranteed.

56. Give presentations to Scout groups.

Scouting is alive and well in the USA.

Tweak your presentation to appeal to your audience and get ready to have a great time. Since many scouting activities are hands-on, you may want to consider gearing your presentation towards a more tactile experience and perhaps help these scouts earn a badge.

A quick call to the Scout Master will help you target your message in an appropriate manner.

57. Give one-day presentations to college students.

College students are an inquisitive crowd. Believe me, they'll keep you on your toes asking questions and soliciting comments you may not anticipate.

That's exactly why you need to present your information to them.

When you do this, you'll not only meet an important demographic group, you'll learn a bit or two about how they think. This is important because as a very strong upcoming demographic with large purse strings, it's to your advantage to get to know these folks. After all, they're fast becoming your next potential customer. They'll buy your books. They'll subscribe to your zine. They're pretty awesome, actually.

You'll also receive another opportunity to tweak your presentations to make them more effective.

To tap into this marketing opportunity, all you need to do is draft a letter offering your speaking skills to your local university. Send it to the appropriate instructors (if you only want to speak to individual classes), or to the event planner if you've got an incredible presentation that is geared towards a huge audience and is suitable for an all-school convocation/assembly. I wouldn't advise this option until you're well into your presentation career. I find my best option is to speak to small audiences and build from there.

58. Tape record your seminars and sell them.

OK. You're busy presenting to civic groups, classrooms full of students, and religious groups. All gratis. What good does that do you?

Well, you're building a ton of credibility. But there's another big benefit you probably haven't thought of yet.

Tape record your sessions and sell them to your mailing list.

Mailing list? What mailing list?

Well... whenever you give ANY presentation, the first thing you do is gather business cards and e-mail addresses. You want to keep in touch with these people on a regular basis. You can easily do this by holding a drawing for one of your books or special reports at the end of your presentation.

After you've gathered these addresses you (or your assistant) will insert them into your database and slowly but surely your list will grow.

Once you've discretely tape recorded your presentation, you can write a killer sales letter selling this recording as a tape, CD, or download, and send this fantastic offer to everyone on your mailing list.

You can also grow your e-mail list the same way. HOWEVER, be sure you have permission to send e-mails to these people. The last thing you need is to be accused of spamming.

Spammers are people who send thousands (if not millions) of unsolicited commercial e-mails to a completely untargeted audience. If you've never received a spam, you're certainly in the minority. I'd venture to guess that our mail Filbert Publishing e-mail addy receives well over 500 spam messages per day.

But I digress....

When you receive an e-mail address from an attendee, before you do anything, send them a quick message asking for their permission to insert their e-mail addy into your database. You can do this by hand, or you can use a free service like Yahoo Groups (Yahoo.com) or Topica (Topica.com) to get them to confirm their desire to be on your list. A paid e-mail hosting service I recommend is Aweber. At these sites, all you have to do is insert the e-mail addy and they'll make sure the potential recipient is contacted and added to the list.

If you send unsolicited e-mails and are accused of spamming, you could lose your ISP, you'll certainly lose the list you've so carefully built, and you can also be subject to fines. But worse of all, you could lose your credibility and any good reputation you've spent years building.

Sending e-mail messages is a powerful tool where you can sell a ton of products. However, never, ever spam.

Building your snail-mail mailing list is fairly easy as well and you don't have to worry about being accused of spamming. The expenses are a bit higher, though.

Weigh your options and use the mix of Internet and brick and mortar promotions that work best for you.

59. Videotape your seminars and sell them.

Once you've perfected your audio tapes, consider videotaping your presentations. This is a more pricey option at this point, but it's certainly doable, especially with technology advancing as fast as it is.

In the past, you could videotape your presentation, transfer that information to another videotape and voila: you've got a product to sell.

Today you can transfer the video information to a DVD. In fact, I've seen machines that will allow you to record directly to DVD, although I haven't seen how the final product looks.

Contact your local access channel to find out what they charge to record your presentation. With this arrangement, you'll probably be able to edit and produce your own line of DVDs and market them to people on your list. You may even be able to compress the file enough to offer it as a download as well.

This project is full of potential. Have fun. Let your imagination run wild. Then get recording.

60. Volunteer.

OK. On the surface, this suggestion doesn't have much in it for you.

However, stick with me a minute.

As a writer, in all likelihood, life has been very good to you.

It stands to reason that when you've been given much, it's only reasonable that you give back as well.

There's nothing sadder than discovering that one of my favorite authors has lost their "edge". Reading their once incredibly inspiring material now feels hollow and dry.

I've always wondered what happened.

Well, throughout these years, I've developed a theory.

It seems that once a writer achieves a certain level of success, it's easy to start believing your own press. Perhaps we start believing that we've got some fantastic "secret" that others must always pay us for. Perhaps we start thinking that we work harder than other writers and deserve success. Perhaps (god forbid) we feel that we're a "level" above everyone else.

I'm not sure how it works but I do know this: when you mentor a student... without pay, mind you... your whole mindset changes. Suddenly you become human again. You realize that public recognition of success ebbs and flows with the tides. And best of all, your able to keep your writing voice as pure as it was in the beginning... full of energy, life, and emotion.

Never hesitate to give back to your community. Take students under your wing. Hammer a nail or two for Habitat for Humanity. Work as a "foster" parent for the Humane Society. Doesn't matter.

Do everything you can to retain your humanity, for your humanity is deeply reflected in your writing voice.

61. Create a scholarship for a high school grad and present it on graduation day.

This one's fun.

Set aside a few hundred dollars to give away to a college-bound high school graduate and set up a scholarship in your or your business' name.

Decide on the criteria you'll use to determine who will receive these monies and then contact your local high school counselor to find out how to get the ball rolling.

Setting up a scholarship isn't nearly as much work as you may think. In fact, you can often coordinate a group of like-minded individuals to contribute so your monetary contribution is quite small.

Make sure your scholarship information is included on the baccalaureate or graduation program. Then imagine receiving free publicity to hundreds, if not thousands of potential clients....

62. Tutor students.

Budget cuts are leaving many school districts staggering under the heavy load of a high teacher/student ratio. It's not uncommon to find well over 30 students per classroom these days!

It's sad.

And what's even sadder is that many of our children are getting lost in the shuffle. And many of these students need extra help but will never receive it.

Businesses like Sylvan Learning Center and Huntington Learning Centers are growing by leaps and bounds. By tapping into a small portion of that market you can add a nice income to your bottom line, keeps your writing skills sharp, and will give you an incredible amount of job satisfaction.

How will tutoring students grow your writing career? Simple.

As a professional writer, you have an edge when it comes to finding those lucky few students you'll be able to squeeze into your schedule. Once parents find out they can have their child tutored by someone who's not just an educator who writes about writing... but someone whose in the trenches and earning a living weaving words together... they'll clamor to try to get their child into your program.

Making this tutoring arrangement exclusive will create buzz. And buzz is one of the best marketing tools you have at your disposal.

Simply slate the amount of time you'll be willing to tutor students. Contact local Communications teachers/professors and give them your business card. You can also mention this limited-space tutoring in your presentations.

Be careful to ride the fine line between working as a writer and becoming a tutor. You don't want a ton of students. However you want one, maybe two, students to make this strategy work.

63. Make sure you give at least ONE handout to every person when you speak to a group.

Always make it effortless for potential customers to contact you.

When you pass out hand-outs at your presentations (and you should always provide hand-outs) make sure your full contact information is on it. Include:

Your name
Your business name
Complete Address
City, State, Zip

Telephone Number
Fax Number
E-mail Address
Website Address
Optional tag line if you want to include one

What do you include in your hand out?

The options are endless.

Provide an outline of your presentation. Give them a tip sheet. How 'bout an article? Booklet? Book? Doesn't matter. Just develop an awesome hand-out filled with useful information that the recipient would be crazy to throw away. And include your contact information.

64. Barter your writing for store visibility.

If you write for a particular audience... and you're lucky enough to know of a particular store or website that caters to that audience, offer to write some of their promotional materials in exchange for a prominent mention, perhaps even an endorsement, to their clientele.

For example, suppose you enjoy writing for the canine agility market. You approach the Bil Jac corporation (this company makes premium dog foods) and offer to write their new brochure. In exchange, you ask that they allow you to piggy-back your solicitation letter inside their next mailing to every store that carries their product. This mailing would include everyone from premium pet store owners to small dog training facilities... your target market.

If they agree to this arrangement, you could have more canine industry people asking you to write their marketing materials than you could ever imagine.

The way to properly work this arrangement is limited only by your imagination.

Contact the big guys in your area of interest and see what transpires. You may walk away amazed.

65. Give away free samples to "sneezers."

Viral marketers call those who engage in heavy word-of-mouth advertising "sneezers." That's because when a "sneezer' gets a hold of a product they love, they'll tell all their friends… and pretty much anyone they come in contact with… how much they love this product or service. And if this sneezer happens to own a publication that gives your writing business a good plug, you could be up to your ears in assignments in the matter of one afternoon. And if their readers are "sneezers", they'll further spread this "virus" until you're completely established and have as much work as you want.

That's why they call this "viral" marketing. The entire life-purpose of a virus is to spread. And you want your writing reputation to spread like a virus… albeit a good virus. ☺

Whenever you write a cool tip sheet, brochure, whatever, make sure to get one in the hands of your resident sneezer. Follow up and see if they'll give it a mention in their publication. Ask them to recommend it to their business friends.

Now isn't the time to be shy. Be bold and ask for what you want. Most likely you'll get it.

66. Hang out where your customers hang out.

Where do your prospective customers hang out? Bowling alleys? Chamber of Commerce meetings? The local animal rights group meeting? How 'bout an Internet message board?

Find your potential clients and participate in their world. Volunteer to serve on committees. Inject information into their discussions. Become passionate about the same causes their passionate about.

I know of more than one writer who has snagged a number of assignments simply by posting a pertinent message on an Internet discussion group.

Yahoo has thousands of groups covering thousands of topics. Find the topics you're interested in and start chatting.

67. Scan the local paper and look for business that would make good customers.

It can sometimes become a challenge to land local writing assignments. However you can easily target your efforts by perusing your local paper.

Chances are that if a local company purchases ad space, they probably have an ad budget.

You want to target companies that understand the importance of reaching their potential customers on a consistent and effective basis.

I often approach these clients and offer to tweak their ads to make them more effective. "You're already paying for the ad to run. Why not get the most bang for your buck," I tell them.

This is a very effective method that has paid off for me. I never purchase a newspaper without cutting out a few ads. You can also dig through your local "Weekly Advertiser", any seasonal publications, and yellow pages to find other potential clients.

You'll find more potential work than you could ever imagine.

68. Create a "blurb" answer to "What do you do" and memorize it.

There's nothing worse than chatting with a fellow business owner and finding yourself unable to articulate what you do for a living.

"So," they ask, "What do you do?"

You smile, gaze into their eyes and say… say… say… WHAT?

Never get caught in this situation.

Take a moment right now and construct a short, clear, coherent, compelling, and benefit oriented answer to that question.

"I write effective advertising copy for businesses who want every promotional piece they distribute to sell their product."

Or how 'bout this:

"I write books that help my readers make their businesses grow."

Anticipate follow up questions and formulate loose answers to those as well.

But most importantly, have fun! Remember, marketing shouldn't be a chore. It's an exciting adventure that'll take you places you could never imagine.

69. Purchase a digital phone so you never miss a call.

I hate hanging around the office when the sun is shining. Most days I've just gotta get outside.

It's for that reason alone that I purchased a mobile phone and use that particular number for all my business needs.

I love to write in the morning. But between 11:00 and noon, you'll always find me outside with my Rat Terrier Wonder Dog, Lucy.

More than once we'll be off on some adventure along the railroad tracks and my phone'll ring.

Another client.

I just smile and take the call loving the freedom this career can provide… if you carefully plan to protect that freedom. Be careful about taking calls after hours, weekends, and holidays or you'll soon become a slave to your phone.

I know of another aspiring writer who purchased a digital phone so he can answer client questions while he's working at his "real" job. He takes a quick message and then calls them back on his break.

I don't advise conducting business on another company's time, however I think it's perfectly fine to answer calls on coffee or lunch breaks. You can also catch up on your calls immediately after work as well.

Make effective use of technology to build your writing business and protect your freedom.

You'll be glad you did.

70. Travel to conventions and seminars and get to know other writers, editors, and publishers.

I'm a horrible introvert. But even I occasionally squeeze myself out of my office and get to at least one writer's convention or seminar per year. And I've never regretted attending any of these events.

I've established life-long friendships at these events. I've met potential clients. I've made valuable business connections that have more than paid for the conference.

But best of all, travel broadens your view of the world and gives you experiences that can make your writing even stronger.

I know it's expensive. I know it's time consuming. But the investment you make in your writing career will pay off.

So grab your mobile phone, hop a plane, and enjoy your adventure.

71. Include a premium with every order.

I'm a strong advocate of multiple income streams. This means that as a writer, you won't just rely on (for example) articles for your income. You'll also receive income from other places like book writing, selling reports, consulting... the sky's the limit.

After we established Filbert Publishing, we found ourselves with some great products that sold at a nice clip.

However, once we developed the "Freelance Pack on CDROM" and offered it as a free bonus to every person who made their purchase directly from us, sales skyrocketed.

So, if you want to perk up response to your marketing, develop a special report and offer it as a freebie to everyone who responds to your ad.

If you want to sell a few more books, offer a free booklet to everyone who contacts you.

Freebies are inexpensive to produce and will pay for themselves many times over.

72. Create a catalogue promoting your other products and send a copy of it with every order you ship.

Once you accumulate a few products you can sell, list them in a catalogue (or on a simple sheet of paper) and mail them with every order you ship.

I'm sure you've noticed that when you purchase something from a big mail-order company, you always receive more promotional materials along with your order.

For example, purchase a book from Amazon, and you'll inevitably receive a flier about a similar book.

Purchase vitamins and you'll receive a new and updated catalogue.

Purchase plant seeds and you'll receive a coupon for a discount on your next order.

This list can go on and on.

You need to do the same thing.

If you completed a writing project for a company, send a discount coupon along with your invoice. Sell a book? Slip a flier inside it listing your other, similar titles.

Never let a prime selling opportunity slip by. Develop your "ride along" promo piece and have it ready for when you need it.

Here are some great promotional tools that we – as writers – are particularly good at:

73. Write a book and get it published.

Nothing builds credibility like writing a book. I have no idea why this happens, but once you've got a book published, the entire world looks at you differently and people suddenly want to work with you.

Crazy but true.

Here's how it works:

Suppose you love the alternative health movement. You'd like nothing more than become a heavy hitter in that field. You've written a few articles for health magazines but haven't had the chance to branch into that field of writing like you'd like to.

So, you sit down and write a comprehensive, yet loose, outline for a potential book. Then you write it.

You start pitching the idea to highly-targeted publishers.

You get your book published.

Now, when you contact potential clients you can say, "I'm the author of "How Wheat Grass Can Cure Your Ills" (OK... I know... the title sucks). This one sentence will open more doors than you can imagine.

I also send potential clients a copy of my latest book along with a letter pitching my writing services to them.

I always keep a book cooking in my mind. Whenever I have a spare minute, I'm feverously banging the keyboard working on it.

You'd be wise to do the same thing.

74. Write a book and *self* publish it.

With today's technology, self-publishing is easier than ever.

You can follow the traditional model of self publishing outlined in Dan Poynter's timeless (and constantly updated) classic, *The Self Publishing Manual.*

You can also use the newest technology called Print on Demand (POD) that will allow you to publish your book and print only the copies you need at the moment.

This means that instead of spending thousands of dollars to format and print your book using traditional publishing avenues, a self-published POD author will spend a few hundred to get their book on the market. Also, many writers have gone the POD route so they can maintain control over every aspect of their career and won't have any third parties owning any part of their works.

To skip so-called "POD Publishers" and deal with the biggest Print on Demand printer in the USA directly (while saving thousands of dollars) I highly suggest you purchase Morris Rosenthal's *Print on Demand Book Publishing.* You can find it listed in Amazon and read excerpts at http://www.FonerBooks.com.

There are up sides and down sides to each publishing method. If you want to learn more you can pick up my book *How to Get Happily Published Without Falling For Scams, Hooks, Lines, or Sinkers.* It's available at FilbertPublishing.com. (Notice the shameless plug?) ☺

75. Hold book signings – and cross promote your business at all times.

I used to hate book signings. The thought of sitting at a little table, pen in hand, waiting for someone to carry their book to me to sign just made my hand tired. Like I mentioned earlier, I'm a hopeless introvert.

However, book signings became much easier for me when I made them reader oriented instead of author oriented. I took time to thoroughly speak to each reader and freely gave them hints to strengthen their ad efforts.

While chatting, I often slipped in references to my other books and more than once received an invitation to visit with them further. These people almost always turned into clients.

Hmmmmm… an avenue where you can "talk shop", chat with business owners, while (with no effort on your part) you are the established expert.

I like those odds.

76. Give away promotional bookmarks – and make sure you include a blurb about your business.

I keep a pile of nice promo bookmarks on my desk. Whenever I mail a special report, book, whatever, I slip on inside. I will even slip one in my direct mail packet and portfolio if I'm in the mood.

Bookmarks with a reader-oriented sales message on them are a valuable sales tool. Just write a short blurb telling your reader how your book/writing services/whatever will make their jobs/lives easier.

Use every copywriting trick at your disposal to turn features into benefits and create a headline that'll make your reader do what you want them to do.

If you're unfamiliar with copywriting techniques, I highly recommend that you purchase Bob Bly's *Copywriter's Handbook* and read it carefully before crafting any ad copy.

77. Give away bookplates – a mini ad placed on each.

If you've published your book and are giving it away as freebies or selling it on your website, a bookplate is an inexpensive and easy freebie to use as a promotional tool to kickstart sales.

What's a bookplate?

It's simply a sticker you place inside the front cover of your book that reads something like this: This book belongs to (your name here).

Some are fancier with Latin phrases and such but you get the drift.

So, you've visited your local print shop and have picked out the bookplate you're going to include as a premium to everyone who purchases your book. What do you put on it?

Well, you include information that'll help your reader find you again. Information like your website address. A one sentence (benefit oriented) blurb.

Your goal is to make it essentially effortless for your potential clients to find you again.

Remember, the world is a busy and loud place. You need to consistently keep in contact with your audience or you risk losing them.

78. Poke a postcard in every book/booklet/info packet you send out.

Filbert Publishing mails a ton of books to Amazon and Baker & Taylor every year. I used to lament that we were unable to add these book-buying customers to our mailing list.

However one day inspiration struck.

Post cards! You know. Those little 5.5" X 4.24" marvels that slip so easily into books?

We now slip one into every book we mail to our wholesalers and distributors. And by golly, we get over half of them back, all filled with buyer information.

We promptly add these names to our mailing list and send them our free quarterly Marketing Journal Newsletter.

Oh… and we also send them our regular promo mailings as well.

It's a win-win situation. We get to keep in contact with a customer we'd otherwise lose, and our reader gets free information and some spectacular deals on our newest and best products.

I highly suggest you implement this strategy into your promo plan as well. It's inexpensive and can reap generous rewards.

79.Send out press releases to newspapers…
80.… radio.
81.… and television stations.

Purchasing ads can get quite expensive.

Imagine receiving a full half page of newspaper advertising your business for free. Or would a 90 second radio spot aired during the prized "drive time" hour suit you? Or how about allowing someone to professionally produce a nice piece about your business (and how it's improving your community) and air it on television during the prime-time dinner hour... at no cost to you?

All these scenarios can easily happen when you learn the fine art of writing and distributing press releases.

The trick to writing a great press release is to (as always) talk about your reader/listener. Then answer these two questions:

Why would your news interest them?

How can you make your information news worthy?

Begin your press release with an attention getting headline. Follow with strong and interesting information that readers/listeners will care about. Then include more specifics pertaining to your story. End with a providing an easy way for anyone listening to contact you.

Four essential elements... no more than one paragraph per element. Never create a press release that exceeds one page.

Once you draft your release, proof it carefully and send it to the appropriate person at every media outlet in your area.

You'll learn something new every time you write a release. Then you can transfer this knowledge to increase response.

Don't expect perfection the first time around. However, do expect that you'll learn a lot.

For further reading: *Filbert Publishing's Jumpstart Your Writing Career* contains step by step instructions on creating a killer press release.

82. Send thank-you notes to EVERYONE who has given you publicity.

Whenever a reporter is kind enough to write a complementary article about you or your writing business, always send them a thank-you card. It's only good manners.

In fact, if you're on the receiving end of a not-so-complementary article… send a "thanks for your time" card as well.

Class always trumps what is probably inaccurate information. ☺

It never hurts to be considerate. It's always right to acknowledge kindness.

Continually spread kindness and the news will invariably bend in your favor next time.

83. Sponsor an event like a read-a-thon, write-a-thon, and donate the profits to charity.

Gather a group of like-minded individuals… perhaps your local writing group… and sponsor one of the above events.

You can pull other people into the event by contacting other writing groups, reading clubs, and teachers to see if their members/students would like to participate.

Print a bunch of pledge sheets, slate the date, and decide who will receive the proceeds. It wouldn't hurt to ask permission from your local city council or state officials to make sure you appropriately follow all the necessary regulations before you start.

The more groups you get to participate the more newsworthy your event will be.

You can raise funds for almost any organization... Habitat for Humanity, Food Shelves, Humane Society... the list is basically endless.

The name of the game is to get your name out in your community as much as possible. Then when they need a professional writer, they'll automatically remember your name.

84. Create a free newsletter.

One way I keep in constant touch with my clients is this: I create a quarterly newsletter and mail it to my clients (and potential clients).

Yes. You're probably already sending your clients your e-mag. However, there's nothing like snail-mail to make sure that your client sees your name on a regular basis.

This project takes some time but is a wonderful way to touch base with your clientele, it will go a long ways towards cementing your reputation as a copywriting expert, and it will serve as a ready-made "portfolio." Clients who receive my newsletter never ask to see a portfolio... they're already acquainted with the quality of my work.

So, here's what you need to do this month... along with sending out your steady stream of sales letters (never forget to do this), develop a newsletter you can send out on a regular basis.

Get to know your desk-top-publishing software. Use a few wizards until you achieve the look you want.

You can also create an "e-magazine." You send this electronic document via e-mail.

I use both a paper newsletter (for my best clients) and an e-magazine to promote my other projects.

That's what's so great about this biz... once you've got your momentum going, the sky's the limit.

And what creates momentum? Action.

So... get to work. Generate some action. Create a newsletter that you can mail to potential clients. You'll be glad you did.

85. Capture every address you can and add to your mailing list.

Record every order you receive in your database program.

Gather addresses from your postcard mailings.

Ask your audience to submit their business cards when you're presenting a speech.

You need to capture every address (and e-mail address) possible so you can build a house list. Your own mailing list is one of your most valuable assets. It's through this list that you can build a strong residual income by offering these people your latest project and you can even rent your list to like-minded companies if it grows large enough..

So, how do you go about getting people to give you their address? Do you say, "I need your mailing address so I can build my house list."

Nope.

You offer them a freebie.

I gather e-mail addresses by allowing my clients/readers to subscribe to Writing Etc., the free e-mag for writers. I gather snail-mail addresses by offering a free quarterly newsletter called the Marketing Journal.

Once you've built your house list, you can offer them products and services on a regular basis. Just make sure you carefully construct your direct mail pieces, test various versions on random chunks of the list, and always tweak your writing style to make sure you're receiving the best bang for your buck.

You also may want to contact your local postmaster to see if you'd benefit from purchasing a bulk mail permit. You can also use various bulk mailers, fulfillment services and mailing list managers to keep your time flexible.

I personally opt to use first class mail. It's well worth the tiny extra cost due to better delivery and open rates.

As you can see, your house list can become an integral part of your writing business. If you haven't already done so, start building your house list today.

86. Give away excerpts of your books.

I think the USA alone houses a gazillion magazines, newsletters, and e-zines.

I'm not kidding. A gazillion. At least.

And every one of these publications are hungry for content.

And why shouldn't you be the person to provide it?

I'd venture to guess that I've given away *Jumpstart Your Writing Career and Snag Paying Assignments* at least four times over. And guess what our best selling book is?

You guessed it. *Jumpstart.*

As you're writing your book, and long after it's published, you can send excerpts to targeted magazines, newsletters and zines in the hopes that they'll publish it in an upcoming issue.

You can use a shotgun method and contact a bunch of publications at once, just make sure that you tell them that you're presenting them a "simultaneous submission." You can offer the excerpts to one publication at a time. The choice is yours.

If you target larger publications, you'll have the best luck offering "First North American Rights" rather than a simultaneous submission. Simultaneous submissions work best for small newsletters and zines.

What you're striving for is to get free publicity for your book. This means that you need to insert your strongest byline at the end of every one of these excerpts. This way the person who reads the snippet from your book will be able to easily find it, and then order their own copy.

87. Keep your book updated – and send out a press release and a mailing to your list EVERY time a new edition comes out.

At Filbert Publishing, nonfiction outsells fiction by at least 50 to one. Of the nonfiction titles, the ones that need occasional updating are our biggest sellers.

It's easy to find a nonfiction subject that need continual updating. Websites come and go. Web pages find new URLs. Government departments are a continual, changing, maze.

Our readers are busier than ever and don't have time to nose all over creation to find the newest and most accurate information.

That's where you come in.

When you write a book that contains information that must be continually updated, you've stumbled on a gold mine.

Here's the scenario: You write the book. Then you sell it, all the while gathering the names of the people who have purchased it. Information changes so you update your book.

After you've updated the information, you send a press release to all your local press announcing that this valuable reference tool is available. You also send a mailing (both snail-mail and e-mail... make sure your e-mail list contains confirmed subscribers only) announcing this new edition.

If you create a thorough and accurate reference book, marketing an annual, semi-annual, or monthly publication can become a strong income source.

88. Create a group or club where potential customers can hang out.

If you love writing for the equestrian market, why not start a local club catering to horse lovers and/or those in the equestrian community?

A monthly meeting of like-minded individuals can become not only a great hobby for you, it can generate exactly the kind of business you're hoping to attract.

As our lives become busy, many people find themselves drawn to niche activities that speak directly to their interests.

You can cash in on this by attracting your audience to events you organize. Don't hard sell at these meetings. However feel free to announce your writing services whenever it's appropriate.

If a similar club/group already exists, by all means join it. But if one doesn't exist, create one. At the very least you'll find out if there's local interest.

If no local interest exists, consider creating a club on the Internet. Yahoo Groups will allow you to do this for free and will give you the tools you need to grow your list.

89. Visit local groups and give presentations.

Never hesitate to accept speaking engagements. I discussed some of these opportunities earlier, but I didn't mention speaking to various specialty groups like the one you just "formed" in the previous tip.

It can be tough to root out some of these specialty groups, but believe me they exist.

Sometimes the only way you can find them is to dig through the local artists directory. Sometimes you simply have to search them out by speaking with other people who share your interest.

Sometimes the local reporter or radio news director may have a lead on whether and/or where these groups meet.

When you find an interesting group, simply contact the person in charge (this can take a bit of work to find this person, too) and offer to speak to their group. Find out how many people attend, what kind of room they meet in, and what kind of visual aids would work best.

A little sleuthing can pay off. Just keep nosing around and you'll eventually hit pay dirt.

90. Be generous with promo copies of your book.

Publishers mail complementary copies of your book to potential reviewers. You must do the same thing.

Send promotional copies of your book to key people in your field who may be willing to give it a mention in their publication or be kind enough to provide you a testimonial.

When an influential person in my field of expertise asks for a complementary copy of my book, I nearly trip over myself to get it to them as soon as I possibly can.

Whenever I find someone in my field who could recommend my book to their readership, I ask if they'd like to receive a complementary copy in exchange for their thoughts (good or bad) about the project.

Receiving even one glowing review from a prominent person in your field will sell more copies than you can imagine. Trick is, you're never quite sure which review will generate those sales. So cover all your bases. If an influential person asks for a comp copy, send them one. Get their reaction to your book, then follow up with a "thank-you" card.

91. Make sure your book has a great cover.

The definition of what a "good" book cover entails changes as frequently as fashion does.

"You can't tell a book by its cover."

Yeah. Right.

While it's true that a cover may not accurately reflect the contents of a book, that same book with a fantastic cover will outsell that same title with a weak one.

So how do you make sure your book receives the cover it deserves?

A great cover isn't cluttered. It's easy to read. It contains a benefit oriented title.

But most of all, it's timely.

Peruse your local bookstore and study the covers. Examine the ones that catch your eye. Also, study the ones that look tacky to you.

When you approach your graphic designer, present them with your ideas and then let them work their magic.

Then be sure to carefully study all your prospective covers… show them to your family and friends… and choose the best one.

Oh, and did I mention that you need your full bio (and maybe your picture) on the back cover?

Never skip an opportunity to engage in covert selling….

92. Hook up with other non-competing yet valuable colleagues and form an alliance.

The writing life tends to be a solitary life. If you're not careful, you may find yourself writing for days on end and never encountering another human being.

That's why it's wise to form alliances with other business owners.

Filbert Publishing has formed alliances with a number of other writing websites. You'd probably think that because it appears as though we're competing websites it wouldn't be in our interest to do this.

You'd be wrong.

Linking with similar websites, working with so-called competing colleagues, and forming alliances with other business owners only strengthens your writing business.

First, you will share some subscribers and web visitors. You can also share products and make extra cash from affiliate sales.

You can also team with businesses that are quite dissimilar to yours but have enough in common that you can profit from these alliances as well.

For example, suppose you owned a writing website and teamed with a website geared towards dog lovers. You can profit from this alliance by offering your writing services to other dog site owners, any dog food reps that may surf by, dog toy vendors… the options are endless.

Never fear forming an alliance with another business. You just may profit from this arrangement PLUS form a lifelong friendship as well.

And don't forget the good old promotional standbys.

93. Advertise in the local paper.

I'll probably sing this song until the day I die: Never underestimate the power of local writing assignments. Local writing assignments will sharpen your talents. They'll teach you how to deal with clients. They'll teach you how to handle cold calls.

They'll teach you more than any writing textbook could hope to.

Placing a small ad in the local paper is a powerful marketing tool.

Couple tricks, though: First, make your ad easy to read. Second, focus on your reader, not your company as you form your ad. Third, make sure you run it on a long term, consistent basis.

You're building a business, not making a quick buck. Always remember this so you continually plant seeds that'll develop into a large harvest later. Newspaper advertising can help you do this.

94. Advertise in magazines.

You can really target your audience by placing a small ad in an appropriate magazine that reaches your particular audience.

If you want to write for direct mailers, an ad in *DM News* could become a highly effective promo tool for you. If you're targeting upholsters, *Upholstery Today* will definitely reach your audience.

A properly constructed ad will pay high dividends. But again, you must run the ad on a consistent basis for it to be effective.

95. Don't forget the Yellow Pages.

Many business people search for suppliers in the local yellow pages. Why not place your ad in the appropriate section?

If you find your yellow page ad does well, you can research regional and even national yellow page directories and see if you'd like to place your ad in these directories as well.

A couple cautions, though. Make sure you're advertising in a legit publication. I know of more than one national "yellow page directory" that's merely a scam designed to rake in ad dollars without actually releasing many books.

Some savvy research on your part will quickly separate the wheat from the chaff in this situation.

However, advertising in your own local yellow pages can become a very profitable investment.

96. Tack your business card to bulletin boards.

When I first started my writing business, I sleuthed around a bit and found out where the business people preferred to eat. I found a fairly upscale restaurant that catered to these people... my audience... and began to frequent it as well.

I also took the extra step of pinning one of my fabulous business cards to the bulletin board directly across from the entrance.

Believe it or not, every time I went back to that restaurant, my card had mysteriously disappeared so I replaced it with a new one.

I've received a number of assignments from that little activity. I suggest you give it a whirl yourself.

97. Write letters to the editor.

One of my favorite pages in the local newspaper contains the letters to the editor. I'm especially pleased when a letter touches upon the nature of doing business in out state Minnesota because it presents me with the golden opportunity of drafting an intelligent and thoughtful response and (perhaps) receiving some free publicity in the process.

Here's how it works: You open your paper and read the letters to the editor. You read this section faithfully until a letter piques your interest. Now you have the opportunity to adding to the dialogue.

Now you sit down at your computer and carefully write a meaningful and thoughtful response. Don't forget to discreetly mention your occupation in your response. Once you submit it (via e-mail or snail mail) sit back and watch your paper to see if you got in.

This method can be a nice way to build a reputation, credibility and a client list.

Couple cautions, though: Be sure to write intelligently. Don't mingle with "hot" issues of the day unless people who respond to those issues are your audience. Keep your letter as positive as possible unless you're fishing for an audience that responds to negativity. Finally, never personally attack anyone. Just write a thoughtful letter that's packed with useful information.

98. Shop locally and talk about your book/business.

I rarely shop outside my community and always strive to shop at locally owned establishments. And while I shop, I always chat with the business owner, slipping in the fact that I write awesome ads that'll increase response rates by a LOT.

Many marketers will tell you to avoid working with small businesses. That may be true if you're working with a small business person you've never met… someone who lives half way around the world from you… someone you "met" on the Internet…but I've found local small business owners a joy to work with.

Never be shy about talking about your writing career. Most people find the subject fascinating, especially when they hear how strong ad copy can improve their bottom line.

99. Cross promote your other products or services every chance you get.

If you want to build a solid writing career with a somewhat predictable income, I highly suggest that you diversify your various sources of income.

Here's what I mean:

You write articles? Great! But what do you do when life gets a little overwhelming and you're not able to pound away at the keyboard for a few weeks? Will your income suffer?

You write ad copy? That's wonderful. But what do you do during any "dry" seasons that may pop up?

Perhaps you're an author. That's fantastic. But how do you supplement your income during seasonal slumps?

The answer to these questions is easy: Diversify.

Pick a few areas of writing that fascinate you. Then develop them. Always keep around three income streams active in your writing life at all times. That way you'll always have a regular flow of cash.

Alone, all these activities I mentioned earlier would produce a pretty spotty income. However, combine them and you can count on a steady stream of paying work.

You can also pitch these various talents to your regular clients as well. Got a copywriting client? See if they need any articles written. Perhaps they need a great graphic designer to lay out their next ad.

Research your options. Develop more income streams and pitch everything you've got to every client you meet..

You'll be glad you did.

100. Promote your other products at the end of EVERY book/article/etc.

Always cross promote your products. If you write an article, make sure you're able to include a fat byline mentioning your current projects, any books you have for sale, and (better yet) your website URL.

Never hard-sell in a byline. However it's perfectly fine to mention any accomplishments, including book titles. Always include a way for your reader to find you. That's why a website addy's so valuable.

Make it effortless for potential clients to contact you, and your workload will skyrocket.

101. Create a nice catalogue.

Do you have a few articles you've written? Turn 'em into booklets.

Got a few longish e-mails you've answered when a reader asks a question? Gather them together and create another booklet.

Once you've got a few booklets and/or reports under your belt, you can create a little catalogue. Once you create this little catalogue (it can be a simple one-page insert) be sure to include it in everything you mail.

If someone purchases a report, slip that little catalogue in with the completed order and you just may experience what experts call a "bounce back" sale.

When you piggyback your catalogue with an existing order, any sales from that little effort are virtually free. You haven't advertised to get that order. You haven't sent a direct mailing. You merely whipped together a few products, slipped a paper into an order, and voila. Another order.

Never send a package without your catalogue. It's like throwing cash out a window when you don't piggyback your efforts.

102. Offer to supply one of your products (books, article reprints, etc.) for fundraisers.

Suppose you have access to a few booklets... perhaps a few copies of your book... for a great price.

You can offer your work for a deep discount (but a minor profit for you) to the organization and allow them to use it in their fundraiser.

For example, suppose you wrote a book about the best camping sites in Northern Minnesota. Now, suppose a Cub Scout pack needed a fundraiser. You call your printer and ask how much he'll need to print a few hundred copies... perhaps even a thousand. You get your price. Now you offer the pack X number of copies of your book to them and tell them they can sell the book for the retail price.

If they take you up on your offer, you can gather the funds, print the books, and deliver them to the scouts.

The scouts raise funds, you receive a slight profit, and everyone's thrilled. PLUS, your name and byline just spread like wildfire.

103. Experiment With Your Promo Materials.

Always tweak your sales materials.

You need to do this because you never want your promo materials to get stale.

That being said, whenever you find a promotional method that works well in landing writing assignments, stick with it.

For example, if direct mail is working well for you, keep sending out letters. BUT, occasionally experiment with a different headline or premium. If you find that it boosts response, keep it. Otherwise, keep tweaking and refining to keep the response rate where you'd like it to be.

Also, experiment with new promo methods. For example, while reading Peter Bowerman's *The Well Fed Writer*, I discovered he liked postcard promos. I'd never used one before, but drafted one on my desktop publishing program. I sent out a few and was surprised at the nice response.

Postcards are inexpensive to make, print, and mail. I'm glad I took his advice and gave it a whirl.

Personality attributes:

Yup. I know. We're sailing right past the 101 point. So consider these final techniques as a gift... at least as important, if not more important, as everything you've read up to this point.

Mindset is everything. If you think you can't succeed, you won't. With just a simple mindset change, your whole personality and outlook on this cool career will change.

And believe me, clients sense true confidence. Negative mindset = few to nonexistent assignments. Great, positive mindset will draw clients towards you.

That's because the positive mindset will trigger an avalanche of activity on your part. Plus, when you finally do receive the assignment, a positive mindset will infuse everything you do for that client with a fabulous energy that's darn near contagious.

And from there your career snowballs.

It's really that simple.

104. Be persistent.

Remember this: If you don't write, you're not a writer.

It's easy to read about writing. It's easy to discuss writing. It's easy to pick other people's writing apart (in fact, sometimes it's downright fun... admit it).

But, you would be surprised that many people who call themselves writers rarely write.

Avoid hanging out on the web too much. Chuck the computer games. Make sure your promotional activities don't exceed a set number of hours each day.

Turn off the TV and read in the evening... you have to read voraciously to be a writer... but don't let reading time eat opportunities to get some writing done.

It's easy to enjoy all the trappings of being a freelance writer... the freedom of a flexible schedule... owning your afternoons... but you're not a freelance writer unless you write. Period.

Once you get cooking on a hot project, keep writing. Avoid interruptions like unnecessary phone conversations so you can keep on track.

Some writers decide how many words they'll write every day, then they stick with it. That way they have a predicable output of writing every day.

Some people are "spurt" writers who are incredibly prolific one day, then are less so the next.

Decide what kind of writer you are, then make a plan that'll work for your style of writing.

105. Be courteous.

In this busy world we live in, it's easy to bypass common courtesy and simply forge ahead.

Despite what you hear and read in popular media, you'll be surprised at how many kind and generous people there are in this world. As you proceed through this crazy profession, you'll be amazed at how many people selflessly help you in every way they can.

The least we can do in return is reciprocate by making our world a little more civilized.

"It's a jungle out there!" "You're swimming with sharks!"

That may be true... but I haven't found that to be in the case of freelance writing.

And when I have run into that very rare "shark", it's usually someone who hasn't acquired much of a portfolio yet.

We're fortunate to be members of an elite, and probably nicer, group of professionals. Perhaps it's our self imposed solitude. But when we finally pull ourselves away from our desks, I've found us to be a generally pleasant and courteous lot.

Let's keep it that way so the next generation of freelancers will discover our culture of courteous helpfulness and carry on the tradition.

106. Be curious.

The main commodity we writers sell is Ideas. Unfortunately, any number of factors can affect the quality and quantity of ideas that pop in our heads.

Get too caught up in promotion... worrying about results, over focusing on it... and you may find your idea pool running dry.

Get to surfing the 'net too much... chatting, checking e-mail, trawling for celebrity gossip... and you could find your creativity decline.

That being said, it's wise to strike a balance between all the activities you need to do to keep your writing business humming smooth and actually writing.

You know you're off track when you hit a writer's block. When you can't write, that means you've allowed your idea pool to dry up. That's when it's time to reevaluate your activities.

But, assuming all is well in your writing life and ideas are flitting around you on a regular basis, that's when it's helpful to keep a notebook handy to keep track of those elusive ideas when they finally come to perch.

So… where do you find ideas?

They're inside you. It's just a matter of jostling them awake.

Begin by surfing to newsgroups to find out what people are talking about.

Read voraciously. Read until something triggers your imagination.

Listen to conversations. (OK… don't be weird about this one… you don't want to be an eavesdropper or anything….)

Talk to people.

Go to the mall and watch what lumbers through.

Write down every idea that flits through your mind, then go back to it later to see if it would make a good book/article/copywriting lead idea.

107. Be professional.

"Hey Beth, since you work at home, do you suppose you can volunteer to head up our {insert worthy cause here}?"

"Nope. I have to work tomorrow."

If I had a nickel for every time I heard that sentence (or one similar to it) I'd be a rich woman. (Please note… if you truly LOVE heading up fundraising events, blood drives, etc., please feel free to do this… but don't take the job unless you want to.)

Yes. We're freelance writers. Yes. We have flexible schedules. We probably write from home.

BUT…

Our job is just as real as a 9 to 5er. If we miss a phone call, we miss an assignment. When we miss an assignment, we miss a paycheck.

When you're a freelance writer, you're self employed. You're a business person. When you take on an assignment you've promised to deliver a quality product, on budget, when your client needs it.

Never miss a deadline. Never charge more than you agreed.

Take this job seriously. If you do this, other people will, too.

That being said, I use a portable digital phone for all my business calls. This allows me the freedom I need to pick up my child from school, go to concerts, or just hang out with him at the Target® snack bar (those cookies are awesome!) and never miss a client's call.

I've found ways to take advantage of my flexible schedule while maintaining the professionalism of having a business phone.

Here's another example:

During the last election, my tiny town couldn't find enough election judges. Because I enjoy the electoral process, I volunteered to help. But to be able to do this, I had to work ahead on all my projects. I contacted my clients to warn them that if they needed any quick rewrites or fast turnaround times on that day, I wouldn't be able to deliver. I also brought my phone with in case they had any questions.

With careful planning, I had a great day at the polls, my work life wasn't interrupted too much, and I felt good about fulfilling a civic duty.

But it was my choice. And any work outside your freelance career should be your choice as well.

108. Create a fair and practical price list.

Pricing is always a snarly issue when a new writer decides to hang out their shingle. I wish I had a nickel for every e-mail I've received asking, "How much should I charge for..."

The best way to create a fair price list is to find out what your competition is charging. As a copywriter, you'll often find these prices higher than you'd expect.

If you can't find any price lists locally, dig around online. Google the word "copywriter" and you'll find more than one price list.

However, without knowing where you live and without knowing anything about your skill levels I can say this: If you're a moderately skilled beginning copywriter, you can reasonably ask for between $40 and $50 dollars per hour to start with. Your prices will rise as your expertise and client list grows.

For a more detailed copywriting price list, you can purchase *Bob Bly's Guide to Freelance Writing Success* and find out what he's currently charging. This book is available in any bookstore or you can purchase it directly from the publisher at FilbertPublishing.com.

109. Network.

Many writers spend far too much time alone.

That's too bad.

The few times I've stuck my head out of my office cocoon, I've been very pleased to find a large group of very helpful and encouraging writers ready to answer any questions I may have about this profession.

Since then, I've collaborated on projects with other writers, I've found a network of professionals I can ask advice, get questions answered, and best of all… I've made some great friends.

You can find these friendly writers online, at writer's conferences, at community education classes, universities, writer's groups, the choice is yours. Just get out there and meet some fellow writers.

Gone are the days of the tortured creative soul… in are the days of living a full, enjoyable life as a writer.

Now get out there and have fun.

110.   Work smart to become the best in your field.

Just like teachers must earn continuing education units to maintain their license, writers must continually educate themselves.

Never slack on your education. It's imperative that you become the best in your area of expertise.

Along with continuing to develop your writing skills, you must create fair, yet speedy turn around times. You must always answer your clients' questions in a thoughtful and courteous way.

Remember, your client always wants the best for their company. You must provide this. And you must help them realize that what you offer is most definitely in their best interest.

Always provide your clients with the best work you possibly can. Never slack off and never allow yourself to be satisfied with less than your best work.

Always present your clients your best timeline. Don't allow yourself to get rushed, but offer a fair and speedy timeline from the first draft to the final copy.

But most importantly, listen keenly to your clients. Often their unspoken words are as important as the ones that escape their lips. A savvy writer will study their clients and give them far more than they pay for and will make their lives much easier in the process.

111. Become a voracious reader.

"If you don't have the time to read, you don't have the time nor the tools to write." Stephan King.

Boy. Mr. King's got this one right.

You wouldn't believe how many writers I've encountered who "don't have time to read."

Poppycock.

If you don't have time to read, you're not a writer. Period.

You need to read everything you can get your hands on. If you write direct mail, read direct mail. If you write fiction, read fiction. If you write nonfiction, read nonfiction.

The average person wastes a lot of time every day. Turn off your TV and read. Place a book on your toilet stool. Stick a book in your car and you can snag a few lines when traffic isn't moving.

Read on your dinner break. Read during supper.

Read while exercising. Grab a magazine when you're waiting for the bus.

Squeeze reading into your schedule everywhere you can.

Your competition probably isn't reading. If you start building your writing arsenal by reading, you'll easily trounce them in every way imaginable.

Oh, and don't forget. Once you're done reading, don't forget to write. Every day.

112. Have fun!

The average person would kill to have our jobs. Here's my typical day:

I wake up when I want to. I work a few hours tapping on the computer keyboard. Late morning, I walk my dear Rat Terrier Wonder Dog.

After dinner, I tinker on a few projects of my choice.

I hang out with my son later that afternoon and eat a nice supper with the family. I spend the rest of my day reading.

How's that for a sweet life?

Well, that life can be yours, too.

Despite the pressure of deadlines, despite the worries of landing clients... writers really do enjoy a flexible schedule. And despite that flexible schedule, I know of too many writers who forget to have fun.

You live once. You only own this moment, once it's gone, it's gone forever.

Every day you live, you choose whether to enjoy it or fret about some small detail.

Believe me, I've spent far too many days fretting over one small irritation or another, but time passes the same whether you worry or have fun.

So choose to enjoy your life and let the little irritations take care of themselves. Because irritations come and go. But loving your life is a lifelong gift.

113. Don't miss a deadline. Ever. Period.

These self-promotion techniques don't take much time. Many are cost-free. The point is that you need to become active in your profession. Writing is as much a profession as it is a lifestyle.

If you're exceedingly introverted (like I am), get over it. You won't make a living as writer if your customers don't know you exist. And remember, it often takes numerous exposures to your sales message before they hire you.

It's a fact of life.

Besides... it's not that bad. The more I promote, the more I enjoy it.

Conclusion

There you have it; more arrows in your quiver than you could ever possibly use.

Latch onto the techniques that fit your personality, turbo-charge your goals, and get you onto the road you wish to travel.

Reserve the rest, don't chuck them, just hold them close. You never know when one of the techniques you thought didn't care for will suddenly become relevant and incredibly useful.

The most important advice I can give any writer is this: the only way to fail is to give up. Once you stop writing, once you tire of promotion, you'll very quickly find your writing career slide, along with your income.

Remain sharp. Embrace life. Achieve the life of your dreams.

About the Author

Beth Ann Erickson is the author of the critically acclaimed novels *The Almach* and *Heart Songs*. Her nonfiction titles include, *Jumpstart Your Writing Career and Snag Paying Assignments*, *How to Get Happily Published Without Falling for Scams, Hooks, Lines, and Sinkers*.

Her articles have appeared in publications like Writer's Weekly, Writing for Dollars, Working Writer's Magazine, and the NAWW e-mag, just to name a few.

Beth works with business owners and entrepreneurs helping them write incredible marketing materials that'll ratchet up their profits to record levels.

Erickson is also the publisher of Writing Etc., the free e-mag that will make your writing sparkle, help you write killer queries, and get you on the road to publication – fast. You'll receive the free e-booklet "Power Queries" when you subscribe.

Appendix A

Bonus: How to Snag $300 For An Hours Work
By Beth Ann Erickson

Ever since Topica changed its format, we've been unable to figure out how to send out our "Welcome to Writing Etc." letter to new subscribers. Because of this, I haven't been able to properly introduce who I am, and what I do.

I figure that's why I received so many e-mails asking, "How on EARTH did you earn 300 bucks for an hours work" after the last issue of Writing Etc. went out.

For those of you who know me, besides running Writing Etc. and Filbert Publishing (which takes less time than it sounds), I also write ad copy for various clients throughout the US.

This is how I make the lion's share of my income. And it's not uncommon to have a client call asking for a quick critique, or even a fast one-page ad.

Because I have a set fee I charge most clients (as opposed to an hourly rate), I sometimes encounter those unique occasions when I'm intimately familiar with the product and can whip out one of these ads in an hour or less.

Ah... that's when I love my hourly wage.

I'm quite amazed that more writers don't branch out into copywriting. The competition (especially on the local level) is basically nonexistent in most areas of the country. It's not a particularly difficult skill to learn. In fact you can learn almost everything you need to know in a matter of a couple months.

Because I receive so much e-mail concerning this subject, I've taken the liberty of answering the top few questions I receive from both students (I'm also a copywriting coach for one of the best copywriting courses available) and subscribers to Writing Etc. Here they are:

1. Do I need super writing skills to be a copywriter?

Nope. In fact, I had to "unlearn" many of the writing rules I learned in college. One of the hallmarks of copywriting is its conversational tone. If you can speak, you can write copy.

2. What if I don't have a college education?

You don't necessarily need it. Although a broad knowledge of a number of subjects is helpful in any profession, it's not always necessary. If you continue your education by becoming a voracious reader, you'll more than make up for that lack of a degree.

3. What was the biggest challenge you faced when you first started copywriting?

Finding clients. However, because I took the time and invested the money to learn some of the insider secrets, I cut the time between finishing the course and landing that first client down by a LOT. Finding local clients isn't as hard as you think. Once you've built a portfolio, landing regional and national clients becomes much easier.

4. Are those high wages (300 bucks an hour) a fluke or are they something I can achieve?

A beginning copywriter can easily charge around fifty dollars per hour. Some copywriters charge by the hour, some by the project. I charge by the project. That way I can make out like a bandit on jobs that take less time than I anticipate. However, the reverse is also true. If an assignment takes more time, my hourly wage is a little less. You can decide how you'll charge your clients. That's the beauty of self employment.

5. How can I become a copywriter?

You can read books. Take courses. Become an apprentice. It's totally up to you.

6. What books do you recommend if I want to start writing ad copy?

The Copywriter's Handbook by Bob Bly
The Online Copywriter's Handbook by Bob Bly
The WellFed Writer by Peter Bowerman
Bob Bly's Guide to Freelance Writing Success by Bob Bly (available September 15)
Jumpstart Your Writing Career by Beth Ann Erickson (Sorry… I just had to plug that!)
http://filbertpublishing.com/jumpstart.htm

7. Any online resources?
Absolutely! The best e-mag I've found is John Forde's Copywriter's Roundtable http://jackforde.com

Bob Bly's e-mag is no slouch either. http://www.bly.com

8. How long until I start earning the big bucks?
That's totally up to you. The more you work in this profession, the higher your wage. If you sit back thinking that clients will flock to your door without any effort on your part, you're probably the wrong candidate for this profession.

However if you're willing to work a little, if you're willing to (as in the immortal words of Ms Frizzle of the Magic School Bus), "Take Chances. Make Mistakes. Get Messy!" you just may do very well as a copywriter.

Appendix B

Here are some websites where you can submit freebie articles. Use these articles to generate free publicity and build your subscriber list.

http://ezinearticles.com
http://www.certificate.net/wwio/
http://www.ideamarketers.com
http://www.marketing-seek.com
http://www.goarticles.com
http://www.netterweb.com
http://www.articlecentral.com
http://homeincome.com/writers-connection
http://www.web-source.net/syndicator_submit.htm
http://www.dime-co.com
http://www.etext.org
http://www.zinos.com
http://www.addme.com
http://www.topten.org
http://www.articlecity.com/
http://www.bestezines.com/
http://www.connectionteam.com/

*These websites are current as of 2006 and may change policies without notice. Be sure to ALWAYS read the terms of use carefully.

Note: Be sure to visit BethAnnErickson.com for all the newest news, cutting edge writing tips, and Beth's speaking schedule. Never know… she just may be coming to your community. She'd love meeting you!

Jumpstart Your Writing Career and Snag Paying Assignments by Beth Ann Erickson

ISBN: 0-9710796-1-7

Think it'll take forever to earn a great living as a writer? Think again.

With Jumpstart Your Writing Career, you'll discover how easy it is to:

- Hone your writing skills until they're razor sharp
- Tackle the most lucrative branch of writing
- Organize your nonfiction articles to make them effortless to sell
- Write powerful queries that'll pull assignments towards you
- Promote your writing business for little or no money

If you want to be a freelance writer who snags paying assignments, this book's for you.

How to Get Happily Published Without Falling For Scams Hooks, Lines, and Sinkers by Beth Ann Erickson

ISBN: 1-932794-13-1

Getting articles and books published today is easier than ever... or is it?

Although new technology has created new writing opportunities galore, it's also created a new breed of publishing that may (or may not) make it easier than ever to make a living (or have a profitable hobby) as a writer.

This book untangles the various options available today to get your manuscript published. We'll also discuss tips to give you the edge when you submit a manuscript, how to spot writing scams, little-known (but profitable) markets that will augment your income as a writer, and much more.

Armed with a little industry savvy, you can not only make a good living freelancing, you can save hundreds (if not thousands) of dollars by avoiding scams, hooks, lines, and sinkers lurking in the world of publishing.

Printed in the United States
56410LVS00002B/277-324